ERIC J. MILLER

Allied We Can Find

COMMON
GROUND

SPIRITUALLY CENTERED PRACTICES FOR
HIGHER-LEVEL LEADERS IN A CONFLICTING WORLD

Published by Eric Miller Consults

Because of the dynamic nature of the Internet, any web addresses or links contained in this book may have changed since publication and may no longer be valid.

Special thanks to Lisa Duncan, editor; and Jen Henderson, cover and interior design/formatting.

Contact Eric at EricMiller.us

DEDICATION

This book is dedicated to all who dare to stand up for what is right, even in the face of opposition. It is a tribute to the courage and integrity of those who choose truth over comfort and action over silence. May this work inspire others to recognize their own power to make a difference, reminding us that real change begins when we have the bravery to defend our shared values.

FINDING COMMON GROUND FOR THE COMMON GOOD

TABLE OF CONTENTS

Chapter 9: Practice Nine, Interdependency   254
Element Four: Passionate and Inspiring

Chapter 10: Practice Ten, Re-purpose   282
Element Four: Passionate and Inspiring

Introduction

A DAY OF THUNDER: THE BOLD SEIZURE OF POWER

THE AIR WAS THICK WITH TENSION as thousands of people gathered, their breaths visible in the chilly air. They had come from all corners, driven by a shared sense of betrayal and a burning desire to reclaim their country. The focal point of their anger was a large, stately building, a symbol of governmental power and authority.

Inside, a meeting was underway. The hall was packed with dignitaries, officials, and citizens, all engrossed in a heated discussion. Suddenly, the double doors at the back of the room burst open with a loud bang, and a man with a stern face and fiery eyes strode in, flanked by a group of followers. His presence immediately silenced the room. He climbed onto a chair, raised his arm, and fired a shot into the ceiling. The sharp crack of the pistol reverberated through the hall, causing people to duck and cover their heads.

"The revolution has begun!" he shouted, his voice echoing off the walls. *"We will not be silenced any longer! Today, we take back our country!"*

The man's followers, numbering in the hundreds, had by now surrounded the building, blocking all exits. Armed and ready for confrontation, they had also taken control of key points within the structure, securing it from any potential escape attempts. Among them were seasoned veterans and fervent supporters, all united under the same banner of change.

The chaos inside the hall was palpable. Officials and dignitaries, some of whom had initially shown support for the man's cause, now found themselves prisoners of the very movement they had hoped to influence. They were herded into a back room, where they were given an ultimatum: join the cause or face the consequences.

As the night wore on, the situation grew increasingly dire. Outside, the streets were filled with supporters chanting slogans and waving flags. They had been galvanized by the leader's fiery rhetoric and the promise of a new beginning. News of the takeover spread quickly, and soon, the entire city was abuzz with rumors and speculations.

Despite the takeover's initial success, cracks began to appear in the plan. The leader had counted on the support of certain key figures, but their loyalty wavered. Some had already begun communicating with the authorities, alerting them to the unfolding events. By dawn, a counterstrategy was in place.

In the early morning light, the leader and his followers decided to march through the city to the main governmental building, aiming to solidify their control. They moved as one, a sea of determined faces, their voices rising in unison. But as they approached their destination, they were met by a formidable barricade of law enforcement officers.

The confrontation was swift and brutal. Shots rang out, and chaos erupted. People screamed and scattered, some falling to the ground. The leader, who had been at the forefront of the march, found himself caught in the melee. He stumbled, his shoulder dislocating as he hit the pavement. Around him, his followers were either retreating or lying injured.

Despite the initial show of force, the insurrectionists were no match for the well-prepared law enforcement. The police had anticipated the march and had positioned themselves strategically to intercept and neutralize the threat. The leader, seeing the tide turn against him, tried to rally his followers for one last push, but it was too late.

By the end of the day, the insurrection had been quashed. The leader and many of his key supporters had been arrested. The building they had stormed had been secured, and the city began to return to a semblance of normalcy. However, the events of that day would leave a lasting mark on the nation's history.

The leader's trial became a spectacle, drawing attention from all corners of the country. His passionate speeches during the proceedings turned him into a symbol of resistance for many, even as he was sentenced to prison for his actions. During his time behind bars, he penned a manifesto, laying out his vision for the future and galvanizing his followers even further.

Though the insurrection failed, it sowed the seeds for future upheaval. The leader's name and cause would resonate in the hearts of many, and the day of the storming would be remembered as the beginning of a new and turbulent chapter in the nation's history.

Do these events sound familiar?

THE BEER HALL PUTSCH: HITLER'S FAILED COUP

In response to the economic and political instability in post-World War I Germany—which had been exacerbated by the harsh terms of the Treaty of Versailles and the hyperinflation crisis—Hitler and his followers, including Erich Ludendorff, attempted to overthrow the Weimar Republic by storming the Bürgerbräukeller beer hall in Munich. Inspired by Benito Mussolini's successful March on Rome in 1922, they believed they could seize power by capturing key government figures in Bavaria and then marching on Berlin to overthrow the national government.

So, on November 8, 1923, the plan was for Hitler and his followers to kidnap Gustav von Kahr, the state commissioner of Bavaria, along with other important Bavarian leaders, and force them to support the coup. Hitler and approximately six hundred stormtroopers surrounded the Bürgerbräukeller, where von Kahr was addressing a large crowd. Hitler burst into the hall, fired a shot into the ceiling, and declared a national revolution, taking von Kahr and his associates hostage.

Despite initial success, the coup quickly unraveled. Key buildings in Munich, including army barracks and communication centers, were not secured, allowing von Kahr and other officials to alert the authorities. By the next morning, the police and military had mobilized to counter the insurrection. When Hitler and his followers attempted to march to the Bavarian Defense Ministry, they were confronted by a heavily armed police force. The ensuing clash resulted in the deaths of sixteen Nazis and four police officers. Hitler was injured and narrowly escaped capture, only to be arrested two days later.

That could have been the end of him. But he used his trial for high treason in February 1924 as **a platform to promote his nationalist** and anti-Semitic views. **This helped him gain publicity, portraying himself as a patriot fighting for Germany's future.** Although he was sentenced to five years in Landsberg Prison, he served only nine months. During his imprisonment, Hitler wrote *Mein Kampf*, which outlined his ideology and plans for Germany. **The failure of the Beer Hall Putsch taught Hitler that power could not be seized through direct action but must be achieved through the manipulation of the political system,** leading to the Nazi Party's **eventual rise to power through legal means.**

MY PATRIOTIC AWAKENING: FROM DISBELIEF TO ACTION

Watching the events that occurred on CNN live on January 6, 2021, I was in disbelief. How could the country that I'd served while in the US Army be in such chaos? A few years earlier, I watched a documentary about the story of Hitler's coup attempt, The Beer Hall Putsch, on the History Channel and thought something like that could never happen in the United States. But it was happening. How could a president who swore an oath to uphold the Constitution possibly go this far to remain in power?

It was at that moment that my patriotic self knew I needed to do something. But what could I do? Albert Einstein said, "If I were to remain silent, I'd be guilty of complicity." So, I had to take some kind of action. I started looking around for ways to have my voice heard. I could rant on social media, and I thought about it but saw how ineffective it was. People on both sides just made things worse, pitting neighbor against neighbor.

Instead, I started writing blog posts and posting articles on LinkedIn. These writings weren't political. They were about what real leadership means to me: a leader who served others and was self-aware, responsible, accountable, compassionate, purpose-driven, and inspirational in uniting people.

COVID-19, the economy, and social unrest that started the pot simmering back in 2014—with the tragic killings of many individuals, including Eric Garner, Michael Brown, Tamir Rice, Eric Harris, Walter Scott, Freddie Gray, Alton Sterling, Philando Castile, Stephon Clark, Botham Jean, Breonna Taylor, George Floyd, Daunte Wright, and Patrick Lyoya—highlighted the deep divisions and unrest within our society. We have certainly been through many challenging times in recent years.

Unfortunately, many leaders weren't unifying the people of the US. There seemed to be a lack of good leadership overall. The articles and blog posts I wrote didn't gain the traction I had hoped they would. So, I started reaching out to people I knew in business to see what they were doing. Opinions were divided: some thought the situation was being overly politicized, while others believed there was clear evidence of wrongdoing. But what could be done to turn things around?

I don't recall any other severe divide like this in the United States in my lifetime. Much of it was due to disinformation campaigns in the public square and on social media. I believe this is the result of fearful people trying almost anything to relieve the anxiety that uncertainty can cause.

What could I do? How could I bridge the divide? Through my network of friends, I found an action group called Business for Democracy based in Columbia, South Carolina. I started attending weekly online meetings.

I was hearing great things from business leaders and politicians trying to make a difference. But the question remained: what could I do? My friend in politics didn't run for re-election because he felt ineffective in the current divisive climate. In my field of spiritually-centered leadership coaching, consulting, and advising, I kept hearing from clients and friends about the strife in office settings. Integrity was on the downswing, and people found it harder and harder to get along at work and at home. Civility was becoming rarer, and it seemed we couldn't even agree on basic facts anymore. Diversity in business was becoming a polarizing issue, with groups and activists on both sides often making things worse despite good intentions.

What could I do? I was getting angrier and angrier, unsure how to make a positive impact without contributing to the hate against the "wrong" group. My spiritual journey over the past nine years had been enlightening. My perceptions of what it means to be a Christian had radically changed. I was starting to see the world in a less and less dualistic way. I have since shifted from seeing life in a simple black-and-white view to an outlook seeing many shades of gray. In other parts of the world, Christianity is growing, while in the United States, it is in sharp decline, while spirituality is on the upswing. Why is that?

HOW DID WE GET TO WHERE WE ARE NOW?

Imagine a group of children playing a game of tag on the playground. One child, eager to win, falsely claims, "I tagged you!" even though they clearly didn't. Some children immediately believe the claim, while others know it isn't true. Instead of continuing the game, the group starts to argue. The children begin to pick sides—some defending the child who made the claim, and others standing up for the one who was supposedly tagged.

Tensions rise as the group splits into factions, each convinced of their own version of the truth. The fun of the game is forgotten, and instead of running and laughing, the children are now engaged in heated disagreements. The divide deepens, and soon, they're not just arguing about the game but about fairness, trust, and whether they can even continue playing together at all.

Usually, in situations like this, an adult—a teacher or playground monitor—would step in. They'd sort out the facts, ask what really happened, and help everyone find a solution that allows the game to resume peacefully. The adult might say, "Let's figure this out together. Was the tag real? Can we all agree on how to move forward fairly?" Their intervention restores the children's focus on honesty and fairness, allowing them to move past the disagreement and enjoy playing together again.

But now, imagine there is no adult in the room—no one to step in and clarify the situation. The children are left to their own devices, and the argument continues. Without someone to guide them back to the truth, the disagreement festers. The group remains divided, and trust among the children begins to erode. What began as a small lie or a simple misunderstanding now threatens their ability to cooperate and have fun as a group. The playground, once a place of joy, becomes a battleground of mistrust.

This playground scenario is a vivid analogy for how disinformation starts small but can fracture relationships, teams, and even societies. Disinformation often begins with a lie or a misunderstanding—something that could easily be corrected if caught early. But when no one steps in to clarify, it grows, just like the children's argument on the playground. People pick sides, trust erodes, and cooperation breaks down. What could have been a simple correction becomes a source of division, just as the children on the playground are now arguing over what is fair and true.

In an ideal scenario, much like the playground, a responsible leader would step in to clarify the truth and correct the misinformation. This intervention could restore trust and allow the group to come together again. But when no such intervention occurs, the disinformation spreads unchecked, just like the children's argument. The longer it lingers, the deeper the divide, and the more difficult it becomes to find common ground.

The issue in today's world is that, too often, there is no "adult in the room." Disinformation goes unchallenged in social media, workplaces, communities, and even in families. People pick sides, and the trust that once held groups together begins to unravel. Leaders and those with authority often fail to intervene, leaving confusion and conflict to grow unchecked. Just like the playground where the lie causes a divide among the children, disinformation fractures societies, organizations, and personal relationships, creating long-term damage.

This book is about navigating different viewpoints and still finding common ground for the common good. It's about having tough talks with people who don't look like us or believe what we believe. It's about connecting with others to have meaningful and purpose-driven lives.

We need to find common ground because we want our children and grandchildren to have the same freedoms we've had and for some to experience them for the first time. So, this is why I'm writing this book. I want to help people integrate the spiritually centered practices that great higher-level leaders have found true for themselves and society throughout history. Traits like being fully present to those around them and being self-aware about who they really are. Having the integrity to stand by their actions, and being accountable when things didn't go as planned. Being vulnerable when they can't do things on their own and reach out for help from someone who does it better. Having the empathy to walk in someone else's shoes and have compassion to act when they see something wrong in the world. Having the ability to forgive well-intentioned people who make mistakes. Being authentic, a "real" person who doesn't "put on airs" so others can feel safe speaking their minds.

A higher-level leader is purpose-driven and does things not just for their own good but to serve others. These spiritually centered people understand that all of us are interconnected, and when "we" harm others, "we" harm ourselves as well. When "we" can be interdependent, "we" can do amazing things. Through understanding and embracing these practices, "we" can hope to bridge the divides that seem insurmountable. This book is my attempt to inspire and guide others toward a more united and compassionate world where true leadership is not about power or dominance but about finding common ground in service, empathy, and mutual respect. *Allied We Can... Succeed.*

Rooted in spiritually centered practices and allied in our quest for common ground, we harness the power of interdependency through higher-level leadership. Together, we achieve what we never could alone.

WHAT ARE SPIRITUALLY CENTERED ELEMENTS IN HIGHER-LEVEL LEADERSHIP?

Throughout my career in various roles and in my personal life, I've faced many challenges that tested my true limits. For instance, there were times when I believed I needed to cover up my mistakes or poor performance. Similarly, I've had people report to me who weren't honest when they missed a goal or made errors, and I had to deal with their standard of integrity. In my personal life, I've lost sight of long-term goals for short-term gratification. Remaining focused despite all the distractions that try to get our attention is challenging in our digital "get it now" world. To add to the complexity of who I am, I can also get tunnel vision and become hyper-focused in achieving goals.

What fascinates me about studying higher-level types is understanding what makes them tick. People who are convicted in their values are the ones who captivate me the most. They are determined to achieve their goals, leaving their mark while remaining true to themselves. These big-picture types excel at communicating their vision. They are passionate about making a difference and leaving an impact on the world. Their dedication to their mission is contagious, inspiring others to join their cause.

I've found emerging themes that separate the ordinary from the extraordinary. It is their adherence to spiritually centered principles. These leaders remain steadfastly true to who they are, even in the face of adversity. Their authenticity shines through, making them stand out. They lead with integrity, compassion, and a deep sense of purpose. This unwavering commitment to their values is what makes them legends and what inspires generations of people.

In shaping my explanation of spiritually centered leadership, I draw inspiration from the Four Elements of Greek philosophy: Fire, Water,

Earth, and Air. The Greek elements symbolize the core elements that guide higher-level leadership and form the foundation of Allied we can...

Element One – Earth: Grounded and Steady

This element symbolizes stability, integrity, and reliability. Spiritually centered leaders foster trust and integrity within their teams, providing essential dependability and consistency. They ensure that their actions align with their words, creating a foundation of trust.

A grounded leader stands firm in their values, creating a secure and supportive environment. This stability is crucial during times of change and uncertainty. A steady, trustworthy leader instills these qualities in their followers.

For example, during a major organizational restructuring, the higher-level leader maintains open communication and consistently demonstrates their commitment to the team's well-being. This approach helps alleviate fears and uncertainties, fostering team members' sense of security and trust.

We will explore how being grounded and steady shapes spiritually centered leadership and offer strategies to build and maintain trust, demonstrate integrity, and provide consistent leadership.

Discussed in: Chapter 1: Practice-Self-Aware, and Chapter 6: Practice-Genuine.

Element Two – Water: Adaptable and Fluid

This element symbolizes adaptability and empathy. Spiritually centered leaders embrace change and encourage open communication, creating a flexible and understanding environment.

Adaptable leaders see change as the only constant. They thrive in it, open to new ideas and perspectives, viewing challenges as growth opportunities rather than obstacles.

For example, adjusting strategies on the fly leads to creative solutions for unexpected problems. When a key project faces roadblocks, encouraging the team to brainstorm alternative approaches can resolve the issue and bring out innovative ideas.

Flexibility pairs with empathy. Valuing others' emotions and perspectives creates a supportive, cohesive environment. Empathetic leaders build stronger relationships and interdependency.

We will explore how adapting to change and encouraging empathy shape spiritually-centered leadership. By embracing these principles, we lead with resilience and compassion, ready to flow through life's ever-changing tides.

Discussed in: Chapter 2: Practice-Mindfulness, Chapter 3: Practice-Vulnerable, Chapter 8: Practice-Validate and Affirm.

Element Three – Air: Visionary and Expansive

This element represents creativity, communication, and expansive thinking. Visionary leaders prioritize clear communication and encourage innovative ideas that drive progress. They see beyond immediate challenges and focus on broader possibilities, inspiring and motivating others with their clear vision and sense of purpose.

Articulating a compelling vision is key. It involves painting a picture of the future and rallying everyone around it. Clear communication provides a roadmap, making the journey more manageable and inspiring.

Expansive thinking is essential. Visionary leaders encourage out-of-the-box ideas, creating an environment where innovation thrives. This empowers team members to contribute meaningfully.

For example, when facing a stagnant market, the higher-level leader adopts an expansive mindset by exploring new solutions and markets. This approach opens new growth avenues and sets them apart from their competitors.

Creating a safe space for experimentation is also crucial. Visionary leaders understand that not all ideas will succeed, but each attempt offers valuable learning experiences. A culture of experimentation empowers teams to take risks and innovate without fear.

We will explore strategies to enhance communication, inspire innovative thinking, and create forward-looking leadership. By adopting the principles of Air, we lead with creativity and clarity, ready to shape the future.

Discussed in: *Chapter 4: Practice-Compassion, Chapter 5: Practice-Forgiving, Chapter 8: Practice-Validate and Affirm.*

Element Four – Fire: Passionate and Inspiring

This element represents passion, energy, and transformation. Spiritually centered leaders ignite passion and drive in others, inspiring creativity and motivation that lead to impactful change. Their enthusiasm is contagious, sparking excitement and engagement, driving their teams to strive for excellence.

Recognizing and nurturing each person's unique strengths is key to inspiring others. For example, in a nonprofit organization, a higher-level leader encourages a volunteer with a talent for organizing events to spearhead a new initiative. This leverages their strengths and inspires other volunteers, boosting morale and expanding the organization's impact.

Passionate leaders create environments where creativity thrives by encouraging dialogue, celebrating successes, and viewing challenges as growth opportunities. They inspire their teams to think creatively and take risks, fostering innovation.

Higher-level leaders develop cultures of collective passion and energy. For instance, a corporate leader might initiate a company-wide "Innovation Challenge" to encourage new ideas for products or services, including workshops, mentorship, and rewards. This fosters a sense of shared purpose and excitement, leading with energy and enthusiasm to inspire transformative change.

Discussed in: *Chapter 7: Practice-Accountable, Chapter 9: Practice-Interdependency, Chapter 10: Repurpose-Driven.*

Chapter 1:
Practice One, Self-Aware

THE SPIRITUALLY CENTERED HIGHER-LEVEL, GROUNDED AND STEADY LEADER

ELEMENT ONE: GROUNDED AND STEADY 🍃

When I was just 19 years old, stationed in Hanau, Germany, I was an upcoming leader and had my first experience of how painful it can be when you don't truly know yourself. I was sitting with Lieutenant Foust, and the room was filled with the kind of excitement you get before big news breaks. *"Miller,"* Foust began, *"I'm putting you in for your third Army Commendation Medal..."* Then he paused, and I could tell something significant was coming. *"...But you're not getting promoted."* The disappointment was almost like something I could touch. *"Woods is getting the promotion,"* he continued. My mind was spinning with questions. *"Lieutenant, why not me?"* I asked. Foust's answer was clear and to the point. *"Miller, you're the hardest worker and always the last to leave. You get the job done, but your team isn't behind you. They feel that they can't trust you. They're uneasy around you."*

He compared me to Woods, who had a different style. *"Woods is getting a medal, too. But his team trusts him. They feel taken care of. If they make a mistake, Woods uses it to help them grow."*

That conversation was a painful pill to swallow. Being passed up for promotion was a tough talk and years later, it was a revelation. Being self-aware would have given me critical information about what I needed to do, but I was young and invincible and thought I knew it all.

MIRROR, MIRROR ON THE WALL: WHO ARE YOU?

Self-awareness is vital for effective leadership. It's the ability to understand your strengths, weaknesses, and motivations, and how these elements impact people around you. When we are self-aware, we can see the truth and take action to change our pathway to achieving our goals when necessary.

Consider my Army leadership experience a cautionary tale: it's not about being the hardest worker or a leader who bosses people around and takes credit for success. It's about connecting with others on a deeper level, showing that you care about their growth and well-being, not just their performance. Listen more, offer support and guidance, and be transparent and honest when things go right and even when they don't.

This shift in approach will gradually build trust with others. When people feel more secure and motivated because they know you have their back, they are more likely to respond positively. Your steadiness and reliability, even in high-pressure situations, will inspire them to mirror those qualities and maybe even more.

Benefits of Self-Awareness:

1. **Enhanced Decision-Making:** Self-awareness helps you recognize when stress is influencing your decisions. By acknowledging this, you'll pause and reflect, considering all options before making critical choices. This leads to more thoughtful and strategic decisions, improving overall performance.

2. **Improved Communication:** Becoming more aware of your communication style reveals that a direct approach may sometimes be intimidating. You create a more inclusive

atmosphere by actively listening and asking open-ended questions, encouraging dialogue and comfortable idea-sharing.

3. **Stronger Relationships:** Self-awareness allows you to understand the importance of empathy in leadership. Regular one-on-one meetings to understand your team's challenges build stronger relationships, increase trust, and create a sense of belonging.

4. **Better Stress Management:** Recognizing your stress triggers and incorporating stress-relief practices like regular exercise and mindfulness breaks will lower your stress level. This also promotes a healthier work environment for everyone.

5. **Increased Adaptability:** Self-awareness helps you identify your limitations during challenging initiatives. Delegating tasks to more knowledgeable team members increases the likelihood of success and highlights your adaptability and trust in your team's expertise.

ELEMENT ONE:
GROUNDED AND STEADY IN SPIRITUALLY CENTERED LEADERSHIP

Have you ever wondered why some people appear comfortable in their own skin, even in tense situations? They know their strengths like the back of their hand, but they're also crystal clear about their flaws, which keeps them grounded. They seem to consistently make the right calls and aren't afraid to seek advice when they don't. These spiritually centered, grounded individuals build a solid foundation of trust and integrity, providing stability and consistency in leading.

This kind of genuineness didn't just happen overnight. People like this, the higher-level leader types, have felt the same setbacks as the rest of us. But here's the kicker: they take brave steps to peer inside themselves, to see the truths, and then figure out their next moves.

Self-reflection isn't a one-off for them; it becomes part of their DNA. They continuously take inventory of themselves through every season. This ongoing practice of self-awareness helps them stay steady and reliable, preparing them for new challenges that come their way.

This journey, this consistent quest of introspection, is crucial and one that I have to make continually. It's about understanding the "why" behind my decisions. Consider it like mining for diamonds, wherein sometimes I find a lump of coal. A leader who is self-aware creates a secure and supportive environment, building trust and consistency with those they lead.

Getting better at this practice is like learning an instrument—it demands patience and persistence. You have to keep asking, "What am I good at?" and "Where did I mess up?" That's the real grind of growth. Continuous self-evaluation builds a foundation of integrity and steadiness that others can rely on.

But self-awareness sometimes means that we have become aware that *we aren't as self-aware as we think*. For example, I had a light bulb moment a couple of years after leaving the service while working at a music distribution company. During a stressful situation, I found myself in a heated argument with my helper, who questioned one of my decisions, blaming it for their mistake. At the time, I was convinced that my anger was justified and that my perspective was the only valid one. However, upon reflection, I recognized that my intense reaction was fueled by insecurities rooted in my experiences as an Army squad leader. The situation had triggered old emotions, even though the circumstances were different. This insight made me realize that my initial reaction was more about my internal state than the external events, highlighting my lack of self-awareness in the heat of that moment.

Being self-aware is about understanding ourselves and how our behavior impacts everyone in our sphere. The more we get to know who we really are, the more truthful we are in leading. Self-knowledge is the real adventure in leadership. Without it, it's like driving in thick fog. But once we grasp who we are, the fog lifts, and we can see the road ahead clearly. Even the big brains at Harvard Business Review back this up, claiming self-awareness is the number one skill for leaders, way more crucial than any flashy degree!

Grounded and steady leadership provides essential stability and consistency. By connecting with the part of us striving for a new way to lead, we'll find common ground with our team and get things done together. It's not ever that we've arrived at being self-aware it's continual introspection. Merge onto the road with me and embrace the adventure of self-awareness.

> Self-awareness gives you the capacity to learn from your mistakes as well as your successes. It enables you to keep growing.
>
> —LAWRENCE BOSSIDY

PAUSE, REFLECT, AND REWRITE: JACKSON'S PATH TO PROFESSIONAL POISE

Jackson was like any other leader in the corporate world. Every day, he walked into his office with a checklist longer than his patience. Meetings, deadlines, targets—they all screamed for his attention. But one day, something changed. He decided it was time to explore a different approach. That was the day Jackson chose a much different response to something that upset him.

Jackson sat at his desk, frustrated. His boss, had made a decision that appeared to be derailing a project, wasting time and resources. Angrily, he began drafting a text filled with his irritation.

Just before hitting send, Jackson paused. He recalled a recent workshop that emphasized reflection before reaction. He decided to step outside for a walk. The cool air helped him clear his mind, and he realized his anger was not just about the decision but also his fear of failure and pressure to meet deadlines.

Returning to his desk, Jackson deleted the angry draft and wrote a calm, constructive text instead:

> *I hope you had a good holiday. I wanted to discuss the recent decision regarding the project timeline. I initially felt frustrated because I believed it cost us valuable time and resources. But I've taken some time to reflect and understand that there might be broader considerations I'm not aware of.*
>
> *Can we schedule a meeting to discuss this further? I'd like to better understand your perspective and share some of my concerns and ideas for future improvements.*
>
> *Thanks*

Jackson's boss responded positively, and they scheduled a meeting. During their discussion, his boss explained the strategic reasons behind his decision, which Jackson hadn't considered. He shared his concerns and offered suggestions for better communication in the future.

The meeting ended on a positive note, with both gaining a better understanding of the other's perspective. Jackson's self-awareness had turned a potentially negative situation into an opportunity for growth and improved team collaboration.

EMOTIONAL SELF-AWARENESS: TUNING INTO YOUR INNER HIGHER SELF

Starting Point: Starter in Emotional Awareness

For those who find themselves at the starting point of emotional awareness, Jackson's story might feel familiar. Much like his initial reaction to his boss's decision, there's a tendency to respond impulsively without fully understanding the emotional landscape. When emotions are only described in simple terms like "bummed," "frustrated," and "angry," it can be easy to overlook the deeper complexities of our feelings. Jackson was so focused on meeting deadlines that he didn't realize how his mindset affected his negative reaction to his boss. His boss's feedback revealed that there were underlying strategic reasons for changing course that Jackson hadn't considered. This stage is often marked by a lack of deep connections and difficulty navigating emotional turbulence, much like Jackson's initial struggle to understand why his anger and frustration affected his relationships at work.

Getting There: Average in Emotional Awareness

As we grow in emotional awareness, we start to sense our feelings more frequently, much like Jackson did during his personal growth in the corporate world. This is a period of ups and downs, where we begin to name our emotions more accurately but might not fully understand their roots. Jackson's realization during the shift in the project direction—when he started to get angry—mirrors this stage. He was aware something was off, but he didn't immediately grasp the deeper issues at play. This level of awareness is about noticing feelings, accepting them, and beginning to explore their origins. It's like going through a familiar routine and starting to pay attention to the subtle changes in dynamics that previously went unnoticed. For example, if you drive the same route to your gym every day. One day, you start noticing small details—like a new shop on the corner, the funny sign at the car wash, or the strange way the light blinks at a particular intersection—that you never paid attention to before.

Aiming High: Exceptional in Emotional Awareness

Reaching a high level of emotional awareness is mastering both the mental and physical elements. People who excel in this area catch on to their emotions quickly and understand their origins. Jackson's journey from focusing on the stress of meeting deadlines to being adaptable to change reflects this. By incorporating mental training and focusing on 'us' rather than 'me,' Jackson began to make better choices with his emotional responses, much like someone who can discern between feeling embarrassed, hurt, or angry and understand why. This level of awareness allows for better handling of stress and more positive interactions, similar to how Jackson paused when he was agitated and placed a higher value on his relationship with his boss.

SELF-AWARENESS:
NAVIGATING YOUR EMOTIONAL TERRAIN

Understanding and enhancing self-awareness is crucial for personal and professional growth. I want to share some valuable techniques that help me to be more self-aware. The following guide will help you identify your current level of self-awareness and provide practical steps to elevate it. By progressing through the learning stages, you'll develop a deeper understanding of your emotions and how they influence your actions and interactions. Whether you're just starting to explore your emotional landscape or looking to refine your emotional intelligence, this guide offers clear, actionable exercises and goals to help you on your journey

1. Starter: Recognizing Emotions

At this stage, recognizing and navigating your inner world is challenging. Strengthening this skill is crucial for developing self-management and social skills.

a. **Self-Awareness Check:** Can you identify simple emotions like happiness, sadness, or frustration as they arise in different situations?

b. **How to Elevate:**

   Goal: *Identify strengths, limitations, and areas for improvement through intentional inquiry and honest evaluation.*

   Tip: Consider seeking 360-degree feedback to gain a comprehensive view of how your behavior affects others. This process involves getting feedback from a wide range of people—such as peers, subordinates, supervisors, and even clients. By hearing perspectives from different angles, you can gain valuable insights into how your actions and behaviors impact those around you, not just from your own point of view. For example, a colleague may notice that while you are very efficient in meetings, you sometimes come across as dismissive without realizing it. The goal of 360-degree feedback is to help you recognize blind spots and areas for improvement that may be difficult to see on your own, leading to more balanced self-awareness and stronger relationships.

   - **Exercise:** Record your feelings in a journal as they manifest in various situations and discuss your findings.

   - **Reflection Question:** *Think about a time when someone asked how you felt, and you replied "fine" or "good" when you weren't. Why did you answer the way you did?*

2. Average: Understanding Emotions

At this level, you can typically recognize your inner world. Further development in self-awareness improves self-management and social skills.

a. **Self-Awareness Check:** Can you explain why you felt a certain way in specific situations and how it affected you?

    Example: When your manager gave you constructive feedback on a project, you felt defensive because you took it personally. This defensiveness caused you to shut down the conversation instead of engaging and learning from the feedback.

b. **How to Elevate:**

    Goal: *Strengthen your understanding of yourself through intentional inquiry and goal setting.*

    Tip: Acknowledge moments of uncertainty, discuss proactive steps, and adapt to situational demands with confidence.

    Example: Rather than reacting defensively to your manager's feedback, you recognized your initial emotional response and took a moment to remind yourself that the feedback was not a personal attack but an opportunity to grow. This allowed you to engage in a constructive conversation and gain valuable insights from the feedback.

    - *Exercise:* Reflect on past experiences and identify emotional triggers and patterns.

    - *Reflection Question: Think about a time when you were surprised at the reaction others had to you—looking back, what caused you to miss their responses at first?*

3. Managing Emotions

You use your understanding of emotions to handle similar situations better, enhancing your self-management skills.

a. **Self-Awareness Check:** Do you apply emotional insights to manage your reactions in new situations effectively?

b. **How to Elevate:**

    Goal: Improve your ability to control and manage your emotions in various contexts.

    Tip: Regularly set and review personal goals related to emotional growth and self-management.

    Example: When confronted by a demanding customer at work, you felt your impatience rising. Instead of reacting with frustration, you applied emotional insight and empathized with the customer's feelings, remaining patient. This approach helped de-escalate the situation and find a solution that satisfied both the customer and the business.

    - ***Exercise:*** Practice mindfulness techniques to stay present and apply emotional insights in real-time.

        o   Daily Reflection Practice: Spend ten minutes at the end of the day reviewing your emotional responses to situations that occurred throughout your day. Notice patterns and triggers and look for ways you can improve.

        o   Journaling: Write about how you managed your emotions and areas where you may have struggled. It is great to have something to review a few weeks later to see where you have grown and where you may need more work.

- **Reflection Questions:**

  Think of a time when you did not feel you had the ability, motivation, and desire to do something difficult. How did you feel and act? What could you do differently next time?

  Which past manager or authority figure has liked you the least, and what would this person tell me about you?

4. Deconstructing Emotions

You can break down your emotional experiences and see their underlying structures.

a. **Self-Awareness Check:** Are you able to dissect complex emotional experiences and understand their components?

b. **How to Elevate:**

Goal: *Develop a deeper understanding of the factors influencing your emotions.*

Tip: Discuss your findings with a mentor or coach to gain additional insights.

Example: After a tense conversation with your brother, you realized that your frustration wasn't just about the topic at hand but also tied to feeling unappreciated in the relationship. When you break it down, you can see that the anger was wrapped up in feelings of disrespect and not being validated, helping you simplify and address the cause of the conflict.

- *Exercise:* Perform a **S.W.O.T.** analysis (Strengths, Weaknesses, Opportunities, Threats) of your emotional responses.

- *Reflection Questions:*

    What five words would you say describe you best?

    Describe a time when your emotions impacted your thoughts and behaviors. What happened? How would you like it to be different in the future?

5. Evaluating: Judging Emotions

You make judgments about your emotional processes and their effectiveness.

a. **Self-Awareness Check:** Can you assess whether your emotional responses are appropriate and effective?

b. **How to Elevate:**

Goal: *Refine your emotional responses based on constructive criticism and self-reflection.*

Tip: Regularly evaluate your emotional growth and adjust your strategies as needed.

- **Exercise:** Seek feedback from trusted friends or colleagues about your emotional reactions.

- **Reflection Questions:**

How have you balanced the priorities of building strong self-confidence with creating strong relationships recently?

Example: Let's say during a work meeting, you noticed yourself becoming frustrated with a colleague's input. Instead of reacting impulsively, you took a moment to assess whether your frustration was justified and how best to respond. You chose to express your concerns calmly, which led to a more productive conversation and collaboration. Upon reflection, you realized that your response helped diffuse tension and resulted in a better outcome for the team.

Think about one of your greatest strengths. How have you used it recently, and what were the results?

6. Exceptional: Innovating Emotional Strategies

Highly self-aware individuals know their strengths and limitations without judging themselves as weak, self-loathing, arrogant, or selfish. They understand their thoughts, feelings, and behaviors and recognize the necessity of self-control. They succeed in group settings and continue to develop this skill through discussion of group dynamics in team settings.

a. **Self-Awareness Check:** Are you able to innovate and create new ways to enhance your emotional well-being? Example: In a high-pressure work environment, you realized your usual stress management techniques were no longer effective. To innovate, you started incorporating short mindfulness breaks during the day, which not only helped you stay calm but also improved your focus and productivity. This new approach enhanced your emotional resilience and positively influenced your interactions with colleagues.

b. **How to Elevate:**

   Goal: *Achieve a higher level of emotional intelligence by continuously adapting and evolving your emotional strategies.*

   Tip: Stay curious and open to new methods of emotional self-improvement.

   - **Exercise:** Discuss group dynamics in team settings to gain insight into yourself through a deeper understanding of others' thoughts, feelings, and motivations.

   - **Reflection Question:** *Think about one of your vulnerabilities or areas of weakness. How has it interfered with the maximum impact of your greatest strengths?*

PRACTICAL STEPS TO ELEVATE YOUR SELF-AWARENESS

1. **Daily Reflection:** Spend 10-15 minutes each day reflecting on your emotional experiences. Write down what you felt, why you felt that way, and how you responded.

2. **Mindfulness Practices:** Engage in mindfulness activities such as meditation, yoga, or deep-breathing exercises to enhance your present-moment awareness.

3. **Emotional Vocabulary Expansion:** Learn new words to describe your emotions more precisely. This can help in better identifying and understanding your feelings.

4. **Feedback Loop:** Regularly ask for feedback from others regarding your emotional responses and interactions. Use this feedback constructively.

5. **Professional Development:** Consider hiring a professional personal coach, taking courses, attending workshops on emotional intelligence and self-awareness to further your understanding and skills.

WELCOMING IMPERFECTION AND PROGRESS

No one is self-aware at all times—it's simply not possible. We all have blind spots and moments when our emotions get the better of us. For instance, even the most seasoned leaders can react impulsively during stressful situations. Being self-aware includes recognizing that we aren't always self-aware. This realization is powerful because it keeps us grounded and open to growth.

Self-awareness is a journey, not a destination. Sometimes the biggest leap in growth can be a step backward before making a step forward. Each step we take, no matter how small, is progress. By understanding and accepting our limitations, we can continue to strive for improvement. Remember, the goal is not to be perfect but to make continuous progress in understanding ourselves and enhancing our relationships with others. Welcome this journey, and you will find that each step brings you closer to a deeper, more fulfilling connection with yourself and those around you.

Alan Mullaly, the CEO who famously brought Ford back from the brink of bankruptcy, credits self-awareness as "the single greatest opportunity for continued growth, performance, and improvement."

JACKSON'S PATH AFTER EMOTIONAL AWARENESS

Jackson's approach to his corporate duties mirrored his approach to life, including his personal relationships. He decided it was time to make some changes. Just like at work, Jackson was often focused on meeting deadlines and managing stress and anger, sometimes at the expense of teamwork and collaboration. In his personal relationships, he reacted impulsively and struggled with frustration. Recognizing these patterns, Jackson knew he needed to continue being introspective.

From the Guide: #1. Recognizing Emotions

It all began with Jackson recognizing his emotions. During his workdays, he made a point to check in with himself. Was he feeling frustrated when he couldn't meet expectations? Was he overly excited when he received praise? Jackson started carrying a small journal as part of his routine. After each day, he'd jot down his feelings. Initially, the entries were simple: "Happy I didn't lose my temper" or "Annoyed by the extra workload." But soon, he noticed patterns. His anxiety levels would skyrocket when his boss made changes to already mapped-out projects, potentially negatively affecting the outcome.

One day, after a particularly tough project, Jackson wrote down his feelings and realized he was not just annoyed—he was scared of failing. That was a breakthrough moment. Recognizing this fear was the first step in addressing it.

From the Guide: #2. Understanding Emotions

With his journal entries piling up, Jackson moved to the next stage: understanding his emotions. Why was he feeling scared? Why did he get so competitive? He started reflecting on these questions during his walks. He remembered how, as a kid, he often felt the need to be perfect while also being the silliest to get attention. This insight helped him see that his fear of failure wasn't just about his job but his need for validation.

Jackson began setting small goals for himself, not just in terms of work performance but emotionally. For instance, he aimed to complete a task without worrying about how he measured up to others. This shift in focus from external validation to internal satisfaction was liberating.

From the Guide: #3. Managing Emotions

Now that Jackson understood his emotions better, he started working on managing them. During work projects, instead of letting anxiety take over, he practiced being fully in the moment, which kept him focused. When he felt the urge to dominate the conversation in meetings, he reminded himself of his goal of supporting his colleagues.

On one critical presentation day, his usual pre-presentation nerves kicked in. But instead of being overly anxious, he took a few deep breaths and visualized a successful outcome. The result? He felt more in control and actually performed better. Managing his emotions helped him stay in the moment and appreciate the experience.

From the Guide: #4. Deconstructing Emotions

With better control over his emotions, Jackson began analyzing them more deeply. He did a SWOT analysis—Strengths, Weaknesses,

Opportunities, and Threats—of his emotional responses. He noticed that his competitiveness was a strength, driving him to improve. However, it was also a weakness when it led to stress and burnout.

Discussing these insights with his coach was invaluable. They talked about his progress and areas where he could still improve. Jackson learned that understanding the roots of his emotions allowed him to address them more effectively.

From the Guide: #5. Judging Emotions

Next, Jackson began to evaluate the effectiveness of his emotional responses. After each project or meeting, he'd review how well he managed his emotions. Did remaining fully present help? Was he able to focus on the task at hand without being overly anxious about his performance?

He sought feedback from his colleagues and coach, who noticed the positive changes. Their input helped him refine his strategies. Jackson realized that even if a project didn't go perfectly, staying calm and supportive of his team was a victory in itself.

From the Guide: #6. The Exceptional Stage

Finally, Jackson reached a stage where he could innovate new emotional strategies. He started using visualization techniques before major presentations, picturing not just success but a supportive and fulfilling experience.

One of Jackson's proudest moments was during a crucial company meeting. Instead of focusing solely on delivering the perfect presentation, he encouraged his team, shared positive vibes, and stayed present throughout the meeting. They performed exceptionally well, not just as individuals but as a cohesive unit.

Through the humbling experiences at work, the stressful projects, and other tough times in his personal life, Jackson got on the path to self-awareness. These experiences taught him to navigate his emotions and understand their impact. But let's be real—he's not perfect, and he's not always self-aware. There are still times when his emotions get the better of him, and he reacts without thinking, or when he falls back into old patterns. It's a continuous journey of growth and learning to be more grounded and steadier. The key is progress, not perfection.

THE WRAP-UP OF HOW SELF-AWARENESS ENABLES HIGHER-LEVEL GROUNDED LEADERS

Reflecting on my youth, I realize that we didn't talk about emotional awareness at all. We were often told not to look inward and not to trust our emotions because they were seen as fickle and sometimes even sinful. This mindset permeated my psyche, making me unaware of how my actions impacted others and myself. It often takes a few knocks or painful experiences to really see what's going on.

In today's world, mindfulness and self-awareness are becoming part of pop culture. However, the lack of self-awareness in many leaders is still evident. Some avoid self-awareness, fearing it might reveal imperfections they perceive as deficiencies. Through his journey, Jackson learned that authentic leadership isn't about perfection but about being honest with oneself, recognizing strengths, and acknowledging weaknesses. The best leaders are those who are spiritually centered. They choose a new mindset pathway, staying fully present, showing vulnerability, and admitting mistakes. They extend compassion to others and are quick to forgive. These leaders are driven by a purpose to make a difference and understand that teamwork is essential for achieving big dreams.

Jackson's transformation began with small steps. He started recognizing his emotions and their triggers, using a journal to document his feelings and reflect on them. This practice helped him see patterns, like how anxiety affected his emotions when his boss made changes to plans. His emotions. Because of the work he put in, Jackson could manage his emotions better, leading to more productive interactions at work.

A significant turning point was when Jackson learned to stay in the moment during critical tasks. Instead of letting anxiety take over, he practiced mindfulness, which kept him focused and calm. This approach not only improved his performance but also his relationships with colleagues. He started setting emotional goals, like enjoying his work without comparing himself to others. This shift from seeking external validation to finding internal satisfaction was liberating.

Incorporating self-awareness and mindfulness into leadership isn't just about personal growth; it's about creating a ripple effect that positively influences everyone. Imagine a world where leaders are aware of their emotions and equipped to manage them effectively. This would result in harmonious workplaces, compassionate communities, and an empathetic society.

The journey to self-awareness and mindfulness is ongoing. It's not about reaching a destination but about continuously evolving and growing. By being honest with ourselves, embracing our imperfections, and striving to improve, we can become the leaders we aspire to be. Jackson's story is a testament to the power of being self-aware and grounded. Allied in this journey, we can create a better, more compassionate world.

"As I have said, the first thing is to be honest with yourself. You can never have an impact on society if you have not changed yourself...Great peacemakers are all people of integrity, of honesty, and humility."

—NELSON MANDELA

RESOURCES

AUTHORS AND EXPERTS ON SELF-AWARENESS

Emotional self-awareness is fundamental to emotional intelligence, enabling individuals to understand and manage their emotions effectively. This collection of insightful books provides an array of diverse perspectives and practical strategies to enhance self-awareness. From scientific explorations and personal development guides to profound insights on trauma and healing, these resources offer valuable tools for improving emotional well-being, fostering resilience, and cultivating meaningful connections.

Know Thyself: The Science of Self-Awareness – *Stephen M. Fleming* explores the latest scientific research on self-awareness, offering practical strategies to understand and manage your thoughts and emotions through metacognition. This book provides a comprehensive guide to the components of self-awareness, enhancing your overall well-being and performance in life.

The Power of Understanding Yourself: The Key to Self-Discovery, Personal Development, and Being the Best You – *Dave Mitchell* provides a clear blueprint for self-discovery and personal development. This book helps readers analyze, understand, and improve their lives through the journey of self-awareness, achieving greater success and happiness.

Self-Care for the Self-Aware: A Guide for Highly Sensitive People, Empaths, Intuitives, and Healers – *Dave Markowitz* offers essential self-care strategies for highly sensitive individuals. This guide provides techniques to manage emotional and physical well-being, promoting self-love and acceptance for those who are empathetic and intuitive.

Trusting Yourself: Growing Your Self-Awareness, Self-Confidence, and Self-Reliance – *M.J. Ryan* provides practical exercises and tools to overcome self-doubt and grow self-reliance. This book helps readers build self-awareness and confidence, empowering them to trust their own judgment and achieve their full potential.

The EQ Edge: Emotional Intelligence and Your Success – *Steven J. Stein and Howard E. Book* provide a comprehensive guide to developing emotional intelligence. This book covers self-awareness, self-regard, and authentic self-expression, offering valuable insights for personal and professional success.

Emotional Intelligence for the Modern Leader – *Christopher D. Connors* teaches leaders the pillars of high-EQ leadership. This guide offers tools and strategies to enhance emotional intelligence, fostering thriving work cultures and organizational success in the modern workplace.

Permission to Feel: Unlocking the Power of Emotions to Help Our Kids, Ourselves and Our Society Thrive – *Marc Brackett* blends scientific rigor with compassion to help readers manage emotions effectively. This book provides a framework for emotional well-being, helping individuals and society thrive through better emotional understanding and regulation.

Happy Life Books: Freedom, Abundance and Fulfillment: Taking Charge of Your Life – *Ayelet Porat* offers strategies for advancing to a life of joy and self-belief. This book combines self-help tools, real-life examples, and scientific evidence to guide readers on a journey of self-awareness and personal fulfillment.

By exploring these books, you can start a meaningful journey toward greater self-awareness. Each book provides unique insights and practical approaches to understanding and managing emotions, ultimately leading to a more fulfilling and balanced life. Whether you seek personal growth, better relationships, or professional success, these resources will equip you with the knowledge and skills to navigate the complexities of your emotional landscape.

Chapter 2:
Practice Two,Mindful

THE SPIRITUALLY CENTERED HIGHER-LEVEL ADAPTABLE AND FLUID LEADER

ELEMENT TWO: ADAPTABLE AND FLUID ⬙

EMBRACE CHANGE AND ENCOURAGE OPEN COMMUNICATION, FOSTERING FLEXIBILITY, AND EMPATHY

The doctor told me, "I can't find anything wrong with you. None of the tests reveal a problem." This was my second such visit in seventeen months. My first scare involved chest pains and numerous tests in the ER, which concluded that nothing could be found. This time, I experienced a startling episode of seeing stars and flashing lights while watching TV, which left me utterly exhausted. After a brief recovery, I drove myself to the ER again, where they diagnosed it to be an ocular migraine. The doctor said, "Eric, this is the second time you've been here in less than a year and a half. These two ER visits look similar in the fact that they both look stress related. I think it's time you made some changes."

Managing Stress, Battling Depression, Anxiety, and Workaholic Tendencies with a Healthy Lifestyle

At the time of the first episode, I was 52. Having been an athlete all my life, I consistently maintained a healthy diet, avoided fried foods, and exercised regularly—I hit the gym twice a week and biked four days a week. I quit smoking at 30 and took up meditation at 47. Despite these healthy habits, I remained a workaholic and I was frequently uptight, struggling to relax when not working. I have battled with anxiety and depression for most of my life. The ingredients of a healthy lifestyle were missing a key ingredient. I had to find another way; what I was doing wasn't working.

In my younger years, I didn't practice mindfulness or understand its importance until the term started appearing everywhere. The doctor's advice hit me hard. It was a wake-up call that despite appearing healthy on the surface, my lifestyle lacked a deeper, essential component. That's when I began to explore mindfulness more seriously. Initially, it seemed like another trend, but the more I looked into it, the more I realized its profound impact on my well-being. Mindfulness, I discovered, was not just about meditation or relaxation techniques. It was a lifestyle choice of being fully present without judging everything. Can you imagine having a way to get through hectic events with a sense of calm and clarity, squashing stress and avoiding the health issues that put the scare in me?

As I embraced mindfulness, I noticed subtle yet powerful changes in my daily life. My morning routine began to include a few moments of quiet reflection, setting the tone for a grounded day. I started doing contemplative sits and mindful walks, allowing myself to connect with my surroundings. Colors seemed brighter, and the air seemed crisper. I was getting off autopilot and actually appreciating more of the little things, like the warmth of the sun on my face during my walks.

Throughout my workday, I started taking brief mindfulness breaks that gave me the opportunity to hit the reset button when tasks and disruptive annoyances drained my energy and focus. At first, I felt like it was a waste of time, but something interesting happened. I got more done because I was more focused and creative. Problems seemed to be easier to solve. These micro shifts made me more adaptable to change. Imagine yourself as a tree, rooted deeply in the earth, able to bend and sway with the winds of change, feeling more flexible and resilient in the face of uncertainty.

The most significant change in me was the way in which I started connecting with people. I became more present and empathetic. When I saw a friend or colleague having trouble getting through something challenging, I would offer a hand to help them out. Mindfulness was helping me to connect on a deeper level, building a sense of trust and unity. I started feeling more grounded when conflict arose, which gave me a better option for responding to tough times. How would it feel for you to be centered in a way that would help you guide yourself and others through the hard stuff?

Although balancing work and family responsibilities is a constant struggle, mindfulness helps me manage the stress. By setting aside time each day for mindful reflection and self-care, I'm able to approach challenges with a clearer mind and a calmer demeanor. Whether it's dealing with the demands of work or navigating personal challenges, mindfulness provides me with the inner resources to become centered.

This shift in me had a significant impact on my physical health. Practicing these techniques helped me listen to my body and recognize the signs of stress before they escalated. Through regular meditation and mindful breathing exercises, I've noticed improvements in my overall physical well-being. This holistic approach to health contributes to my mental and physical resilience.

Imagine the impact your ability to be empathetic and grounded could have, not only on your leadership but also in reducing stress. Did you know that prolonged stress significantly impacts lifespan? Studies from Yale say that we can shave off almost three years of our lives if we live in a constant state of fight or flight. I know my body was screaming at me to do something different, and do it now. How about you?

Mindfulness is simply being aware of what is happening right now without wishing it was different; enjoying the pleasant without holding on when it changes (which it will); being with the unpleasant without fearing it will always be this way (which it won't).

—JAMES BARAZ

THE CRAFT OF MINDFULNESS IN HIGHER-LEVEL LEADERSHIP

Meet Emma, a project manager who worked with Jackson. Emma was always a perfectionist, thriving on meticulous planning and flawless execution. However, recent project delays and unexpected changes started to wear her down. Her once dynamic, take-charge demeanor turned into a daily slog. Meetings that used to be her playground now felt like marathons. The constant setbacks and shifting deadlines chipped away at her enthusiasm, leaving her bogged down by negativity and low energy. Emma, who once handled challenges with ease, found herself struggling to keep her head above water as the weight of perfectionism and unpredictable project hurdles took their toll.

The Wake-Up Call

It all started on a Tuesday morning. Jackson had just wrapped up a meeting that felt more like a battle. Emma's negativity and low energy was sucking the air out of the room. After the meeting, Jackson called Emma into his office.

"Hey, Emma, got a minute?" Jackson called out, a friendly smile on his face.

Emma nodded and plopped into the chair across from him, sighing heavily. *"Sure, what's up?"*

Jackson leaned back in his chair, taking a deep breath and pausing while he organized his thoughts. Then he said, *"Emma, you know I think you're one of the best project managers we've got. But lately, it seems like your attitude has gone south, and I'm feeling your negativity."*

Emma's eyes widened, a mix of surprise and embarrassment flashing across her face. *"What do you mean?"* she asked, her voice defensive yet curious.

Jackson chuckled softly, trying to keep the mood light. *"Look, I get it. We've had a rough few months with all the project delays and unexpected changes. But I've noticed you're not your energetic self, and it's starting to affect the team."*

Emma frowned, sinking a bit deeper into her chair. *"I know, Jackson. It's just been so hard to stay upbeat with everything that's been going wrong."*

Jackson nodded sympathetically. *"I understand, believe me. But here's the thing—you're a perfectionist, and that's great for project execution. However, it also means you take these setbacks really hard. Can I offer you a suggestion that could really help you?*

With a cynical smirk on her face, she said, *"Sure?"*

"Have you ever tried taking a few minutes to just breathe and reflect?"

Emma raised an eyebrow. *"You mean like meditating?"*

"Not exactly," Jackson replied, leaning forward with a playful glint in his eye. *"Think of it as a quick reset. When things get overwhelming, take five minutes to step outside, find a quiet spot, and just focus on your breathing. Let your mind wander to something positive, like a favorite memory or something you're looking forward to. It helps you recharge and reset your attitude."*

Emma's interest was piqued, though she remained skeptical. *"And you think that will help me turn things around?"*

Jackson grinned. *"Absolutely. It's like hitting the pause button on your stress. It can shift your perspective and restore your energy. Plus, you might find it easier to tackle those project hurdles with a fresh outlook."*

Emma hesitantly smiled, feeling a spark of hope. *"Alright, Jackson, I'll give it a try. I could definitely use a mental reset."*

Jackson laughed. *"That's the spirit! And remember, it's not about being perfect—it's about looking at these obstacles as opportunities to be excellent on a new pathway. You've got this, Emma."*

As Emma left Jackson's office, she felt a lightness she hadn't experienced in weeks. Maybe this simple practice was exactly what she needed to reclaim her enthusiasm and lead her team with renewed energy.

The New Morning Ritual

Emma would sit quietly in her office every morning before anyone else arrived. She focused on her breath, feeling the rise and fall of her chest. Those five minutes soon became her sanctuary. She noticed that starting the day with a calm mind set a positive tone for everything that followed.

One morning, as she sat in silence, she realized something profound. Emma had been so caught up in the hustle that she had forgotten to truly listen—not just to her team, but to herself. This was her first lesson in mindfulness: the power of presence.

Positive Shifts

As Emma became more mindful, she noticed changes both in herself and in her team. During meetings, she practiced active listening, giving her full attention to whoever was speaking. This simple act made her team feel valued and heard, and they became more engaged and motivated.

Emma also started incorporating short mindfulness exercises into meetings. Before diving into the agenda, they would spend a minute in silence, focusing on their breath. It initially felt strange, but soon, it became a cherished ritual. The team noticed that their meetings were more productive and less stressful.

The Stress Buster

Leadership often meant dealing with high-pressure situations, and Emma was no stranger to stress. One particularly tense day, with a crucial deadline looming, she felt the familiar knots of anxiety tightening in her stomach. Instead of reaching for her usual cup of coffee, she decided to take a mindful walk. As she strolled through the park near the office, she noticed the chirping birds, rustling leaves, and children's laughter. These simple, serene moments allowed her to release worries and fully embrace the present, feeling more accepting of the recent changes in the project requirements.

When Emma returned to the office, she felt refreshed and ready to face the challenges with a clear, positive mindset. She approached her team with a renewed sense of openness, encouraging them to share their concerns and ideas freely. Reminding herself of the talent and capability within her team, she knew she could trust them to work together and find a solution.

Building Strong Connections That Matter

Being fully present helped Emma understand and bond with the team. This deepened empathy, built trust, and strengthened their relationships, creating an interdependent, motivated group. Think of a mentor guiding their mentee, ensuring they have the support and resources to thrive. Emma practiced mindfulness by listening attentively to the team during strategy sessions. Her genuine interest in the thoughts and feelings of her colleagues set the stage for entrepreneurialism.

A calm and focused mind is more open to new ideas. Mindfulness encouraged creative thinking and problem-solving by allowing Emma and the team to step back from immediate concerns and view challenges from a broader perspective. When the team seemed to be stuck on a particular hurdle, Emma would lead a short stretching break with the group. This technique has an incubation effect on the brain wherein the creativity gates would open up stimulating creativity and innovation within the group.

Authentic Leadership

Mindfulness also taught Emma the importance of authenticity. She realized that being genuine in her interactions built deeper connections with her team. Instead of trying to appear invincible, she shared her challenges and vulnerabilities.

During a team meeting, Emma opened up to the team about her journey with mindfulness. *"I was letting all the pressures of deadlines and changes in the project direction overwhelm me,"* she admitted. *"But practicing mindfulness helped me find clarity and calm. I'm still learning, and I appreciate your support."*

Her honesty resonated with the team. They saw her as a whole person, not just their team lead. This authenticity created a sense of trust and respect.

Higher-Level Strategic Planning

Integrating mindfulness into strategic planning enables us to think more clearly, collaborate more effectively, and navigate challenges with greater ease. It empowers us to create comprehensive, adaptive, and ethically sound strategies that drive our long-term success.

When we include mindfulness, we create space to reflect deeply on our objectives and the steps needed to achieve them. This reflective practice helps us identify potential obstacles and consider various perspectives, leading to more well-rounded and robust plans. For instance, a mindful approach to strategic planning might involve setting aside uninterrupted time to meditate on our desired outcome, allowing insights to surface naturally and inform our decisions.

The Impact of Mindfulness on Personal Lives

Mindfulness isn't just an inner resource for professional settings; it also profoundly impacts our personal lives. When we practice mindfulness, we become more aware of our own needs and those of the people around us, deepening connections.

Mindfulness can be integrated into various aspects of life, from daily routines to specific situations. Starting the day with a mindfulness meditation or a few minutes of deep breathing sets a calm and focused tone. We can also insert mindful eating during lunch or taking a mindful walk. For instance, Emma begins her day with a short meditation, which helps her approach tasks with clarity and purpose. She also practices mindful breathing during breaks, ensuring she stays centered throughout the day.

Practicing mindfulness helps us stay present and fully engaged. This means listening without interrupting, being aware of body language, and responding thoughtfully. When we make a point to focus fully during social gatherings, acknowledging each speaker with undivided attention, it significantly improves understanding and unification.

When conflicts arise, as they often do when strong personalities are together, a mindful approach can make a significant difference. We can use mindfulness to stay calm, understand different perspectives, and find equitable solutions.

We often face immense pressure, leading to stress and burnout. Mindfulness provides a healthier way to manage these challenges, such as recognizing early signs of stress, practicing self-compassion, and taking regular breaks to recharge. By integrating mindfulness into our daily routines, we decrease stress, acknowledge our limits which helps us set healthy boundaries, and take time to relax and rejuvenate, maintaining energy and focus while avoiding burnout.

Making Change Less Scary

Change is inevitable in every facet of life. We better tolerate change by staying present. Mindfulness helps us remain grounded and focused on the present moment rather than getting lost in worries about the future or regrets about the past. This approach helps maintain stability during uncertain times. By embracing mindfulness, we navigate transitions with greater ease, adaptability, and a positive outlook, ultimately improving our overall well-being and effectiveness.

The Role of Mindfulness in Our Culture at Work and in Our Communities

Mindfulness isn't just a personal tool; it has the power to reshape organizational and societal cultures. When leaders prioritize adaptability and empathy, they set a positive example that encourages a culture of cooperation. When leaders are mindful, employees feel valued and heard, boosting their motivation and productivity.

On a broader scale, mindfulness bridges societal divides. Employees who practice mindfulness bring these skills into their everyday lives, enriching their interactions with presence, empathy, and thoughtful communication. Imagine an employee who listens attentively at work and then takes that same attentiveness into their community activities. This kind of engagement strengthens community bonds and enhances local problem-solving.

Picture a city where mindfulness is the norm. People approach public issues with calm and clarity, leading to more productive discussions and creative solutions. Mindful citizens help build a society that is resilient, responsive, and adaptable to change.

REFLECTING ON EMMA'S JOURNEY

Maybe you're not an executive. Perhaps you're a different kind of leader—a teacher guiding students, a parent raising children, or a community organizer bringing people together. Whatever your role, I hope there's something in Emma's journey that resonates with you. Her story of embracing mindfulness helped her overcome negativity and deepened her relationships.

Being present enhances our ability to lead effectively, regardless of the setting. Think about the moments when you feel overwhelmed or disconnected, and consider how mindfulness could help you navigate those challenges more clearly and calmly.

Is there something that stands out to you about Emma's story? These experiences are not unique; they're part of the human experience. By integrating mindfulness into your daily life, you, too, can become grounded and calm. Embrace mindfulness not just as a practice but as a way of living and leading, and watch how it impacts the world.

The best way to capture moments is to pay attention. This is how we cultivate mindfulness. Mindfulness means being awake. It means knowing what you are doing.

—JON KABAT-ZINN

FROM THE FRONT LINES:
REAL STORIES OF MINDFUL LEADERSHIP

As we've seen in Emma's story, mindfulness can profoundly impact performance. Many real-life leaders have successfully integrated mindfulness into their leadership practices, demonstrating its tangible benefits in the business world. Let's explore the stories of Janice Marturano and Alan Mulally, two leaders who have made mindfulness a keystone of their leadership and corporate strategies.

Janice Marturano: Cultivating Mindfulness at General Mills

Janice Marturano, former Vice President of General Mills, successfully incorporated mindfulness into her leadership and the corporate culture. Under her guidance, General Mills implemented mindfulness programs that improved employee focus, clarity, and creativity, enhancing decision-making and overall performance.

Marturano's journey with mindfulness began as a personal endeavor to manage stress and find balance. Recognizing its potential to enhance corporate culture, she pioneered mindfulness programs at General Mills. Starting with small workshops, these initiatives expanded company-wide, teaching techniques like mindful breathing, meditation, and mindful listening.

The notable Mindful Leadership Program combined mindfulness practices with leadership training to cultivate self-awareness, emotional regulation, and a deep sense of purpose among leaders. This improved communication and collaboration, resulting in higher engagement, creativity, and job satisfaction.

Marturano's efforts showed that mindfulness is a strategic tool that can reshape an organization's culture and performance. General Mills' accomplishment inspired other companies to adopt similar programs, validating the impact of mindfulness on business success.

Alan Mulally: Mindfulness Played a Role in Ford's Comeback

Alan Mulally, the former CEO of Ford Motor Company from 2006 to 2014, used mindfulness to lead the company through one of its toughest periods. During the 2008 financial crisis, when Ford was on the brink of bankruptcy, Mulally's calm and focused leadership was instrumental in steering the company back to profitability. By practicing mindfulness, he remained composed and made clear-headed decisions, which was crucial during the high-pressure moments of restructuring the company. His ability to stay present and thoughtful allowed him to navigate complex challenges without becoming overwhelmed.

Mulally's commitment to mindfulness didn't stop at his own practice. He also encouraged his team to adopt mindfulness techniques, resulting in a culture of openness and trust. Regular mindfulness practices, like starting meetings with moments of silence, helped everyone stay focused and aligned with their goals. This approach boosted morale and enhanced teamwork and collaboration, which were key factors in Ford's successful turnaround.

The impact of Mulally's mindfulness on Ford's success is undeniable. His mindful leadership style created a positive work environment, reducing stress and improving overall productivity. By staying present and empathetic, Mulally built stronger relationships with his team, leading to better communication and more effective problem-solving. His mindful approach proved that staying calm and collected, even in the face of adversity, leads to remarkable success.

Mindfulness helps you go home to the present.
And every time you go there and recognize a condition
of happiness that you have, happiness comes.

—THICH NHAT HANH

INTEGRATING MINDFULNESS INTO HIGHER-LEVEL ADAPTABLE AND FLUID LEADERSHIP

In my quest to make positive changes in my lifestyle, I've discovered several practices that not only enhance personal well-being but also elevate leadership effectiveness. These practices are simple yet profound, focusing on being fully present, engaging deeply with your surroundings, and responding to situations with clarity and calm. Higher-level leaders, like Janice Marturano and Alan Mulally, have integrated these techniques into their leadership styles with remarkable success. Embedding these practices into your routine will help to improve both personal and professional relationships.

Mindfulness practices, such as deep breathing, meditation, and mindful listening, dramatically impact the way you lead. Commit to giving them a go, and you'll see what I've been talking about throughout this chapter.[1]

---

[1] Disclaimer: *The information provided is for educational purposes only and is not intended as a substitute for professional medical advice, diagnosis, or treatment. Always seek the advice of your physician or other qualified health provider with any questions you may have regarding a medical condition. Never disregard professional medical advice or delay in seeking it because of something you have read in this book. If you have a history of mental health issues or trauma, please consult with a mental health professional before starting any new meditation practice.*

I've learned that personal discomfort can be a powerful catalyst for change. Experiment with different mindfulness techniques to avoid them becoming a chore. The only mistake is not starting them.

All Ears: Tuning In with Wholehearted Listening

Ever find yourself nodding along in a conversation while your mind races? Or crafting your next reply before the other person finishes? We've all been there. Here's a mindset shift: wholehearted listening. It means paying full attention—no distractions, no planning your response. This superpower enhances relationships, showing you genuinely care. It roots you in the moment, leading to deeper connections and more interesting conversations. Next time you chat, catch yourself drifting and refocus. Wholehearted listening is your secret to making others and yourself feel awesome.

Pen to Paper: The Magic of Journaling

Ever felt like your brain has too many tabs open? Journaling can help close a few. Writing down your thoughts helps you explore feelings and sort through thoughts, often revealing new insights. I prefer pen and paper rather than typing for a genuine experience—just you, paper, and pure reflection. Start simple: jot down dreams, joys, or annoyances. Each page lightens your load, helping you discover yourself. So, grab a pen and let your journal capture your story, one thought at a time.

Breathe Easy: The Simple Science of Focused Breathing

I used to smoke because it calmed me, partly due to the increased air intake. Have you noticed how a few deep breaths can clear your mind and reduce stress? That's focused breathing!

Focused breathing involves slow, deep breaths, like filling and deflating a balloon. It centers your thoughts and brings you to the present moment.

Eric's Coaching Tip

Sit comfortably, inhale slowly through your nose for 4 seconds, hold for 4 seconds, then exhale through your mouth. Repeat ten times. Use this technique to calm yourself anytime.

Find Your Zen: The Magic of Guided Meditations

Ever thought about trying meditation but weren't sure where to start? Guided meditations might be your ticket to inner peace—and it's easier than you think!

Guided meditations are like having a personal coach in your ear, with calming music or soothing sounds. They help you focus, breathe, and stay on track. There are apps for all devices, offering sessions for relaxation, focus, or sleep. A few minutes of guided meditation daily can bring more relaxation and clarity into your life.

Spot Check: The Lowdown on Body Scans

Ready to get in tune with your body? Let's talk about body scans—a meditation technique to connect with your body from head to toe.

Here's how it works:

Lie down comfortably, start at your toes, and mentally scan your body upward. Focus on each part, noticing how it feels without trying to change anything.

Why do this?

It's like taking inventory of your body. This practice increases awareness of any aches or tensions and is deeply relaxing. It helps release unnoticed tension, leaving you lighter and more relaxed. Try a body scan to wind down or reset your day.

Stretch and Flow: Unleashing the Power of Yoga and Tai Chi

Have you ever considered trying yoga or tai chi? These practices blend movement, breathing, and awareness, offering a workout beneficial for both brain and body.

Here's the deal:

Both practices focus on flowing movements and breath. Yoga enhances flexibility and calmness, acting as a reset button for stress. Tai chi, known as meditation in motion, involves slow, precise movements and is great for balance and stress relief. Suitable for all ages, these practices clear your mind and promote peace. Roll out a mat or clear a space and discover the mental clarity and strength yoga or tai chi can bring.

The Power of Doing One Thing at a Time: Single-Tasking Magic

Ever feel like you're spinning too many plates at once? Between texting, emails, projects, and meetings, it's easy to feel overwhelmed. Single-tasking can save the day!

Single-tasking means committing to one task at a time. In our hyper-connected world, it's a radical idea! This practice reduces stress, enhances efficiency, and lets you enjoy tasks more fully. Focusing on one task allows deeper understanding and higher-quality work.

Eric's Coaching Tip

Concentrating on one task at a time helps you complete it faster and with fewer errors. Next time you're multitasking, try single-tasking. Choose one task, eliminate distractions, and watch your efficiency soar,

Now You Sense It:
Embracing the Full Spectrum of the Moment

We often go through the motions without noticing our surroundings. It's time to try sensory engagement, which involves immersing yourself in the present by tuning into all your senses.

Imagine walking in a park. Instead of zoning out, notice everything: the green grass, rustling leaves, earthy scent of soil, rough tree bark, and a faint taste of mint from your toothpaste. Sensory engagement grounds you in the present, making it hard for your mind to wander.

Eric's Coaching Tip

When overwhelmed, take a sensory inventory. What can you see, hear, touch, taste, and smell? This simple practice pulls you back from stress and helps you find calm. Engaging your senses not only helps you relax but also enriches your life. Be in the moment and let your senses lead to a more vibrant, mindful life.

Chew on This: The Delights of Mindful Eating

Ever caught yourself munching on snacks without really tasting them? It's time to try mindful eating—fully experiencing your food.

Mindful eating involves slowing down and paying attention to your meal. It's about savoring each bite, noticing flavors, and tuning into how the food feels.

Here's how you do it:

Next time you eat, look at your food and notice the colors and smells. Chew slowly and think about the taste and texture—is it salty, sweet, crunchy, or smooth? This transforms eating into exploring.

Mindful eating helps you eat less and enjoy more. Slowing down allows your body to signal when it's full, reducing overeating and encouraging you to choose satisfying, nourishing foods.

Go Wild: Unplugging and Recharging in Nature

Experience the rejuvenation of "Nature Time." Exploring places like the desert southwest and northern forests taught me the power of the wild. Embrace the outdoors, whether scaling trails or biking through forests, to reconnect and find serenity. Nature renews, making you part of the landscape, a reminder to shake off those worries. When life feels overwhelming, turn to nature. A hike, bike ride, or sitting by a stream can reset your perspective and recharge your spirit.

Roll and Stroll: The Mindful Way to Move

Turn your daily walk or bike ride into a mini vacation for your mind. Mindful walking or biking is about more than just commuting; it's about fully experiencing each moment. Feel the rhythm of your steps or pedals, tune into surrounding sounds, and notice your breath. This practice clears your mind and sparks creativity, providing a mental break from screens and schedules. Challenge yourself to soak in every part of the journey for a fresh perspective.

Taking a Break from the Digital World

Our world constantly buzzes with notifications. Ever wonder if it's too much? A "digital detox" helps find balance—not quitting technology but taking breaks. Try to spend weekends off social media or commit to no emails after dinner. Remember when tech promised more free time? Now, it demands our attention 24/7. Aldous Huxley warned of endless diversions controlling us. Always being connected hinders enjoying the moment. Try turning off notifications or a screen-free Sunday to reduce stress and enhance connections.

GET MORE DETAILS ON MINDFUL LIVING

Unlock a deeper sense of presence and clarity in your life by visiting our mindfulness resources. Simply scan the QR code to explore valuable insights and practices that can help you cultivate a more centered and balanced mindset. Don't miss this opportunity to take a step toward greater peace and focus.

bit.ly/mindfulpract

END OF THE CHAPTER,
BUT THE BEGINNING OF BEING FULLY PRESENT

I used to think mindfulness was just a quick fix for stress. But through my experiences, I've realized that mindfulness is a lifestyle that influences every part of who we are and how we interact with the world. As Martha Beck wisely said, "How you do anything is how you do everything." This philosophy is at the heart of mindfulness. It's about bringing intention and presence to every action, no matter how small, and recognizing the profound impact it has on our lives and those around us.

Reflecting on my health scare, it was a wake-up call that made me reassess my approach to stress and well-being. Those moments in the ER, with the doctor telling me it was all stress-related, were pivotal. They pushed me to explore mindfulness beyond just meditation, to embrace it as a holistic approach to living. My hope is that you don't get to the point I did.

Let's reflect on Emma's story. Imagine yourself as Emma, a project manager facing the daily grind of deadlines and shifting priorities. Perhaps you've felt the weight of negativity and low energy, just as she did. Now, envision the change that comes with embracing mindfulness. By integrating mindfulness into her routine, Emma became more adaptable and fluid, handling changes gracefully. Picture yourself developing a heightened awareness and presence, staying calm under pressure, and making more thoughtful decisions. This shift didn't just improve Emma's well-being; it had a broader impact on her entire team. Her newfound flexibility and empathy created a positive, collaborative environment. Imagine your leadership style evolving, creating an environment where people actually want to be there with each other, no less.

Change never happens unless it's too painful to remain the same. In many ways, it was too painful for me not to change. Practicing mindfulness makes a profound difference. I've witnessed it many times, and the contrast is shocking.

Making meaningful changes in ourselves is often the first step toward improving our interactions and relationships. It's true that you can't give away something you don't have. To offer calmness, empathy, and presence to others, we have to first cultivate these qualities within ourselves. By practicing mindfulness, we can develop a deeper self-awareness and emotional regulation, allowing us to be fully present in every moment. This presence sends a powerful message that we truly care about the people and situations around us.

Consider the impact of calmness on your pet dog, Fido. Animals are incredibly sensitive to human emotions and energy. When you are calm and present, Fido senses this and feels more secure and relaxed. Your mindful presence creates a more peaceful environment for both of you, strengthening your bond. The ripple effects of mindfulness extend to every aspect of our daily interactions.

What if you paused and responded calmly instead of reacting with anger when someone says something that upsets you? Mindfulness teaches you to take a moment to breathe and reflect before reacting. This practice disarms tense situations and leads to more constructive conversations.

Consider how these techniques could change your perspective on politics and religion. By being fully present and open-minded, you engage in conversations about these often contentious topics with a sense of calm and empathy. Mindfulness allows you to listen more deeply and respond more thoughtfully, creating understanding and respect even when you encounter differing opinions. This approach leads to more meaningful and productive dialogues, helping bridge divides and building stronger connections with others, regardless of their political or religious beliefs. By staying calm and composed, you demonstrate maturity and control, which defuses conflicts.

Road rage is another area where mindfulness can make a significant impact. Practicing mindfulness teaches you to stay present and focused, reducing the likelihood of becoming overwhelmed by frustration or anger while driving. This makes the roads safer and reduces stress levels, making your commute a more pleasant experience and perhaps even lifesaving.

Imagine a life where you don't need to rely on alcohol to unwind after a stressful day or coffee to get through the morning. Mindfulness helps you to be fully present in the moment and is a natural way to combat depression and manage anxiety. Through mindful breathing and meditation, you'll achieve a state of calm and alertness without external stimulants. This shift not only benefits your physical health but also your mental and emotional well-being. Mindfulness helps you connect with yourself at a deeper level, allowing you to make strides in adopting a growth mindset and turning challenges into opportunities for personal development. Additionally, mindfulness practices can be a great addition to therapy for trauma recovery, providing a supportive foundation for healing. By embracing mindfulness, you will cultivate a more balanced and fulfilling life where calmness and clarity replace the need for temporary fixes and lead to lasting well-being.

Mindfulness is not only a practice but also a spiritual element of higher-level leadership with the ability to impact the whole world. Allied, we can find common ground to build stronger, more empathetic connections. By being fully present and engaged, we send a powerful message to those around us that we genuinely care about their well-being and success. This mindful presence creates a ripple effect, inspiring others to adopt the same approach and contributing to a more productive world. Embracing mindfulness in leadership is the key to creating lasting positive change on a global scale.

Mindfulness is the key to effective leadership.
You have to be present to lead.

—BILL GEORGE

In a busy vintage record shop, Alicia and Marcus found themselves grabbing for the same album. They struck up a conversation about the band they both loved and decided to go next door for a cup of coffee. As the conversation continued, they shifted from music to world events and it quickly became apparent that while they shared musical taste, they held starkly opposing political views. What began as a casual chat soon turned into a heated exchange, with Alicia's voice growing louder and Marcus' frustration mounting.

But before the situation could escalate further, Marcus remembered his commitment to mindfulness and self-awareness. He noticed the anger rising within him and paused to take a deep breath, grounding himself in the present moment. Speaking calmly, Marcus acknowledged their differences and made a conscious decision to listen without judgment. This approach caught Alicia off guard. She had been ready for a verbal battle but rather than continuing to push her point, she tried to understand his position.

As the tension eased, neither of them changed their minds, but they were both more open to the conversation. Instead of trying to win the argument, they both started to share their perspectives, not to convince the other but to understand. By the time they finished their coffee, they had found mutual respect and a sense of connection, recognizing that a civil conversation was stronger than a bitter disagreement.

RESOURCES

AUTHORS AND EXPERTS ON MINDFULNESS

There are many renowned experts on mindfulness who have contributed extensively to the field through their writings and teachings. Here are some of my favorite key figures who have authored popular and influential books on mindfulness:

Jack Kornfield – A trained psychologist, Jack Kornfield is one of the key teachers who introduced mindfulness practice to the West. He has written many books, including *"A Path With Heart"* and *"After the Ecstasy, the Laundry."*

Jon Kabat-Zinn – A pioneer in making mindfulness accessible to Western audiences, Jon Kabat-Zinn founded the Mindfulness-Based Stress Reduction (MBSR) program at the University of Massachusetts Medical School. His books include *"Full Catastrophe Living"* and *"Wherever You Go, There You Are."*

Saki Santorelli – He succeeded Jon Kabat-Zinn as the director of the Center for Mindfulness in Medicine, Health Care, and Society at the University of Massachusetts. His book *"Heal Thy Self"* speaks to the experience of teaching and practicing mindfulness.

Richard Rohr – A Catholic Franciscan Priest offers 366 daily reflections drawn from his extensive writings. His book *"Yes, And... Daily Meditations"* The meditations are organized around seven themes, blending Scripture, tradition, and personal experience to deepen Christian faith in a spiritually enriching way.

Eckhart Tolle – Known for his teachings on presence and spirituality, Eckhart Tolle's books, such as *"The Power of Now" and "A New Earth,"* focus on the importance of living in the present moment.

James Finley – As a former monk and student of Thomas Merton, Finley offers practical guidance on meditative practices to deepen one's spiritual connection with God. His book *"Christian Meditation: Experiencing the Presence of God"* provides an introduction to the practice within the Christian tradition.

Thich Nhat Hanh – A Vietnamese Zen master and peace activist, Thich Nhat Hanh has written extensively on mindfulness and meditation. His works include *"The Miracle of Mindfulness"* and *"Peace Is Every Step."*

Sharon Salzberg – A central figure in bringing mindfulness and loving-kindness meditation to the West, Sharon Salzberg has authored books like *"Real Happiness"* and *"Lovingkindness: The Revolutionary Art of Happiness."*

Andrew Newberg and Mark Robert Waldman – *"How God Changes Your Brain"* reveals the impact of spiritual practices like meditation on brain health. It combines neuroscience and survey data to show that such practices can enhance mental and emotional health, modify brain functions, and alter perceptions and values.

Daniel Siegel – A clinical professor of psychiatry at the UCLA School of Medicine, Daniel Siegel writes about mindfulness and the intersection of neuroscience and human relationships. His books include *"Mindsight"* and *"The Mindful Brain."*

Susan Stabile – She was a Buddhist monk for over a decade before returning to Catholicism, authored, "Growing in Love and Wisdom" The book offers practical guidance on using Buddhist meditation techniques within Christian meditation, highlighting the enriching potential of interfaith dialogue and shared spiritual truths.

Pema Chödrön – An American Tibetan Buddhist, she is known for her accessible teachings on mindfulness and dealing with difficult emotions. Her books include *"When Things Fall Apart"* and *"The Places That Scare You."*

Tara Brach – A psychologist and proponent of Buddhist meditation, Tara Brach blends Western psychology with Eastern spiritual practices. Her books, such as *"Radical Acceptance"* and *"True Refuge,"* focus on using mindfulness to address emotional pain and suffering.

Ruth Haley Barton – Founder of the Transforming Center, shares practical steps and reflections to help individuals reconnect with God and themselves. *"Invitation to Retreat: The Gift and Necessity of Time Away with God"* guides readers through the practice of spiritual retreats. This book highlights the profound benefits of intentional solitude and spiritual renewal.

These authors write about mindfulness and offer practical guidance and exercises to cultivate a mindful lifestyle. Their books are a great resource for anyone interested in deepening their understanding and practice of mindfulness.

Chapter 3:
Practice Three, Vulnerable

THE SPIRITUALLY CENTERED HIGHER-LEVEL ADAPTABLE AND FLUID LEADER

ELEMENT TWO: ADAPTABLE AND FLUID ⬙

EMBRACE CHANGE AND ENCOURAGE OPEN COMMUNICATION, FOSTERING FLEXIBILITY AND EMPATHY

Growing up in a small conservative midwestern town in the 1970s and early 1980s, people viewed vulnerability as a weakness, not a strength. Showing any sign of softness or emotional openness was often met with criticism or, worse, pity. This mindset shaped me a lot. I learned to put on a tough exterior, hide my fears, and always present myself as having all the answers, confident and in control. In my young mind, it didn't occur to me that being vulnerable was courageous.

As I grew older and took on leadership roles, this facade of invulnerability stuck with me. I thought that to be an effective leader, I needed to be flawless. I had to be a rock for others. But this approach started to take its toll. Deep down, I felt inauthentic, and it disturbed me.

The turning point came when I met a leader who completely changed my view on vulnerability. His name was Walter, and he was the regional sales manager at a music distribution company where I worked. What struck me about Walter was his openness and authenticity. He wasn't afraid to share his struggles, admit his mistakes, or ask for help. At first, this baffled me. How could someone so openly vulnerable command such respect and loyalty?

One day, during a particularly challenging project, Walter gathered the team and shared his own doubts about a project's success. He spoke honestly about his sleepless nights over whether we could meet our goal. In a way that felt like he was including us in the decision-making process, he laid out the hurdles and the possibilities for moving forward. As a group, we brainstormed his ideas and gave our input. Collectively we found a solution and created a new strategy that turned out to be the ideal pathway to an even better outcome. We were going to achieve our goal and, in the process, solve another issue the company was having.

Instead of seeing him as weak, I saw him as incredibly brave. His honesty created a space where the rest of us felt safe to share our ideas. It built an environment of trust and teamwork that I had never experienced before. This really opened my eyes to a new way of viewing vulnerability in the workplace.

SETTING THE STAGE FOR VULNERABILITY AND SUCCESS

Imagine a leader who says, *"I'm not sure, but let's figure this out together,"* or *"I made a mistake, and I need your help to make it right."* That's the leader who wins hearts and minds. That's a courageous person.

The power of vulnerability goes beyond building trust and effective teams. It also cultivates compassion. When we are open about our struggles, we create a space where others feel safe to do the same. This mutual sharing builds a compassionate environment where people are more willing to help each other. It shifts the focus from individual success to collective well-being, which is an element of spiritually-centered leadership.

Daniel Goleman teaches that knowing our feelings and understanding others' emotions are keys to being real and influential leaders. By being vulnerable, we inspire others to do the same, creating a ripple effect of authenticity and trust that recalibrates teams, organizations, and communities.

Are you saying to yourself, "Yeah, right, Eric! I tried that a long time ago, and it resulted in disaster."

Many people think being vulnerable at work is like walking a tightrope. They worry that opening up about their struggles might be seen as a sign of weakness, leading to judgment or loss of respect. For example, a boss might hesitate to share personal challenges, fearing their team will question their leadership ability or competence. They might avoid talking about their need for help on a project with colleagues, concerned it could be seen as a sign they can't handle the workload or the stress.

And then there's the fear of betrayal. Sharing personal struggles can backfire. A leader might be honest and have it used against them and spread as gossip. Or they might divulge an idea about making the company more money only to have a colleague take the idea and say it was theirs.

On a more personal level, they might have shared a controversial belief with a friend and lost the friendship. Or a friend promised to keep a secret and didn't. Or maybe a family member rejected them after revealing something sensitive.

I get it. All of those things have happened to me. But here's the thing: *when done right,* vulnerability is courageous and can actually bring us closer and strengthen relationships. A manager who admits to struggling with work-life balance might encourage their team to share their own challenges, leading to collective solutions and increased empathy. A colleague who talks openly about their learning curve on a new project inspires others to seek help and collaborate more. Friends who share their personal struggles deepen their trust and understanding of each other, building a stronger support system. Even family members benefit from open communication, finding better ways to support and love each other.

It took me a long time to understand that there's a *right and wrong way* to be vulnerable. Being vulnerable is *not about exposing every detail* of our lives; it's about being honest and real. It's about showing our true selves in a *general way,* admitting that we don't have all the answers, and being open to feedback and support. Brené Brown, one of my favorite wise people on the subject of vulnerability, teaches us that showing parts of our true selves—our worries and our wins—makes our connections with others deeper and our lives richer. Embracing vulnerability requires adaptability and fluidity, allowing us to navigate uncertainties with grace. Open communication, grounded in authenticity, further strengthens these bonds, creating a foundation for understanding and collaboration.

I started being vulnerable the smart way and being real with people. It was terrifying at first. I remember the first time I admitted that *"I didn't know"* and needed help. I expected people to lose confidence in me, but the opposite happened. They appreciated my honesty and rallied around me, offering their perspectives and support. This built a deeper sense of trust and interdependency.

COURAGEOUSLY VULNERABLE WITH WISDOM

Working with Walter at the music distribution company inspired me to emulate him. His openness and authenticity were huge for our team. He built trust by sharing his challenges and acknowledging errors and turned those experiences into valuable training opportunities. Additionally, his transparency created a safe space for seeking help.

With Walter's influence and my experiences in mind, I'll divulge more about the character Jackson that I shared with you in the first chapter. By the way, Jackson, Emma, and soon-to-be-introduced

Sarah are all characters based on coworkers and people up to the present day. The challenges that I've written about and the ones coming in later chapters are real events that I participated in or observed firsthand.

Jackson was becoming more mindful, and his stress levels plummeted. He was managing his emotions and pausing while agitated before responding. He was more at ease with himself than ever before, and others noticed the remarkable changes.

Jackson was eager to deepen his connection with his team but struggled with how much to share. He had great ideas that came from past experiences but was hesitant to reveal them out of fear of ridicule and his team losing respect for him. Jackson also had concerns about someone possibly stealing his ideas and taking credit for them. After getting over those legitimate concerns, he tested out being vulnerable at work but lacked the experience to execute, and the result was less than awesome. That event made him fearful of ever trying it again.

Staying vulnerable is a risk we have to take if we want to experience connection.

—BRENÉ BROWN

JACKSON'S STRUGGLES WITH VULNERABILITY: SETTING BOUNDARIES FOR BEING VULNERABLE AND MAINTAINING VULNERABILITY

In his younger years, Jackson had been a "keep it to yourself" kind of guy, especially in the workplace. He believed that showing any sign of vulnerability was a weakness that could be exploited. He kept his personal life strictly separate from his professional one, wearing a mask of unwavering confidence. But one day, in a moment of uncharacteristic openness, he decided to share something personal—and it went horribly wrong.

It all started during a brainstorming session earlier in his career as a marketing coordinator. The team was stuck in a rut, and their ideas weren't flowing. Hoping to break the ice, Jackson said, *"You know, guys, I've been feeling pretty down lately. My girlfriend broke up with me, and I've had a tough time moving on."* The room fell silent. His colleague, Karen, raised an eyebrow and said, *"This isn't the time for personal issues, Jackson. We need solutions, not problems."*

Jackson felt his face burn with embarrassment. His colleagues avoided eye contact, and the atmosphere grew colder. That moment haunted him, reinforcing his belief that vulnerability had no place in the office. From then on, Jackson became even more guarded, determined never to let his personal struggles show again.

A few years later, Jackson found himself in his role as a CTO at a tech company. He had perfected the art of maintaining a professional facade, but he noticed something was missing. The team was struggling to accomplish a project with many design changes wherein they would restart segments that had just been completed, with deadlines not commensurate with the workload. His team's morale and performance were down, and irritability was at an all-time high. In the past, they had been efficient, but lately, everyone was distant, each person siloed in their tasks with a lost sense of camaraderie. He couldn't help but feel responsible for the lack of connection.

One day, during a leadership workshop, Jackson encountered the concept of vulnerability as a strength. The charismatic facilitator shared stories of leaders who transformed their teams by embracing vulnerability. Intrigued but skeptical, Jackson decided to give it another shot. He planned to start small and see if it could make a difference.

In the next team meeting, Jackson took a deep breath and shared a carefully considered personal insight. *"I want to talk about something that's been on my mind. I've been struggling with imposter syndrome lately, feeling like I'm not doing enough as a leader. It's been tough, but I'm working on it."* He made sure to keep it relevant to their work, framing it as an effort to improve his leadership.

To his surprise, the response was overwhelmingly positive. His team members, rather than recoiling, leaned in. Emma, the project manager, spoke up, *"I've been feeling the same way with the project that seems to have requirements that I haven't seen in a while. It's reassuring to know I'm not alone."*

Another colleague added, *"Jackson, I feel you. When I first started here, I felt the same way—like I was never good enough. It was overwhelming."*

Yet another team member chimed in, *"I've felt similarly when dealing with tight deadlines. It can be so stressful."*

Jackson nodded, taking in all their comments. After everyone had shared, he asked, *"Thank you all for sharing. Would it be okay if I share my experience and how I've addressed similar challenges?"*

The team nodded, showing their interest and support.

Jackson began, *"Emma, if I'm hearing you correctly, you said that you felt the same way when taking on a project that you haven't seen in a while, is that correct?* Emma nodded. Jackson went on,

"When I first encountered a project with unfamiliar requirements, I felt overwhelmed too. I've found that breaking down the tasks into smaller, manageable parts and seeking input from the team really made the process less daunting. Does that help?"

Turning to his colleague who mentioned feeling like they weren't good enough, Jackson said, *"I've felt that same pressure, especially when I was new."* The new colleague gave a thumbs up. Jackson continued, *"We're super glad that you're here, and you're doing a great job. What I found helpful was to focus on the progress I was making, no matter how small. Celebrating those small wins built my confidence over time. Thank you for sharing that with us."*

Addressing the team member who was dealing with stress from tight deadlines, Jackson nodded and said, *"Oh yes, I've certainly felt my share of stress due to tight deadlines."* The colleague nodded. Jackson continued, *"When I've felt that way, I found that setting small, achievable goals really helps me stay on track and manage the stress better. It's something I've learned through experience, and it's made a big difference for me."*

Jackson finished by saying, *"Thanks, everyone. It means a lot that you all could open up, I hope this helped. We all have our challenges, but by sharing, we can find ways to overcome them together. Let's continue to support each other like this."*

Encouraged by this experience, Jackson continued to explore the balance of vulnerability and professionalism. He introduced weekly "Check-In Chats," where team members could share their thoughts and feelings about their work and any challenges they faced. These sessions were a hit, creating an environment of trust and mutual support.

One memorable moment was when Jackson shared a story about a failed project from his past. *"I once led a campaign that flopped spectacularly. It was a huge blow to my confidence, but it taught me valuable lessons about planning and resilience."* His honesty inspired others to share their own stories of failure and growth, transforming the team's dynamic into one of openness and learning.

Jackson's journey from an Emotionally Zipped-Up Leader *to a* Leader in Emotionally Out-there Mode wasn't easy, but it paid off. His team became more cohesive, innovative, and supportive. Regular feedback sessions ensured that the practice of vulnerability was sustained and appreciated. Jackson acknowledged and celebrated team members who bravely shared their stories, reinforcing the importance of this newfound openness.

In the end, Jackson discovered that *when balanced with professionalism*, vulnerability could transform a team. His journey taught him that showing his human side didn't make him weak; it made him relatable and trusted. By unlocking the power of vulnerability, Jackson created a work environment where everyone felt valued, leading to greater connection and collective success.

Transparency doesn't mean sharing every detail.
It means sharing the things that matter.

—SIMON SINEK

When *done appropriately*, inserting vulnerability into your leadership style will positively impact your work environment and any other professional setting, for that matter, into a space of trust and collaboration. This guide is designed to help you balance openness with professionalism. You will create a supportive team dynamic by setting clear boundaries, practicing active listening, and fostering a culture of mutual respect. Below, you'll find practical steps and exercises to help you and those you lead grow stronger together. Explore and see how vulnerability leads to greater connection and success in your environment.

Part 1: Setting Boundaries

This step focuses on establishing clear boundaries about what is appropriate to share within a professional setting. Sharing personal challenges and how they impact work can help open up emotionally while maintaining professionalism.

Goal: *To create a safe environment where leaders can share personal insights without compromising professional integrity.*

Application Example:

Jackson began his professional journey believing that personal issues should be kept private. After a negative experience in which a colleague dismissed his vulnerability, he closed himself off. However, Jackson later learned to balance openness and professionalism. In a team meeting, he shared a relevant personal insight: "I've been struggling with imposter syndrome lately." This helped his team see him as relatable while respecting professional boundaries.

Exercise:

a. **Identify Personal Boundaries:** Reflect on your personal life and identify challenges that affect your work.

- Jackson began his professional journey believing that personal issues should be kept private. After a negative experience in which a colleague dismissed his vulnerability, he closed himself off.

b. **Determine Appropriateness:** Decide what aspects of these challenges are appropriate to share in a professional context.

c. **Share with Context:** Share the selected personal insights with your team, ensuring to frame them in a way that maintains professionalism. For instance, explain how a personal issue has influenced your focus at work *without delving into excessive details.*

- Jackson later learned to balance openness and professionalism. In a team meeting, he shared a relevant personal insight: "I've been struggling with imposter syndrome lately." This helped his team see him as relatable while respecting professional boundaries.

Reflection Questions:

1. What personal challenges have I faced that have impacted my work?

2. How can I share these challenges in a way that is appropriate and professional?

3. How did my team react to my sharing? Did it change the team dynamics? Better? Worse?

Part 2: Practicing Active Listening

This step emphasizes the importance of stepping back and listening to your team members. Active listening involves fully concentrating, understanding, responding, and remembering what the team members are sharing. This is one of the mindfulness practices discussed in Chapter 2.

Goal: *To build trust within the team and encourage team members to share their own challenges and ideas.*

Exercise:

a. **Initiate Listening Sessions:** Set up regular meetings dedicated to listening to team members. Ensure that these sessions are focused on hearing their thoughts, challenges, and ideas.

b. **Demonstrate Active Listening:** Show that you are actively listening by nodding, maintaining eye contact, and not interrupting. Summarize what the speaker has said to confirm understanding.

c. **Ask Open-Ended Questions:** Encourage deeper conversation by asking open-ended questions that prompt team members to elaborate on their points.

Reflection Questions:

1. How often do I practice active listening with my team?

2. What have I learned from my team members by actively listening to them?

3. How has active listening affected my relationship with my team?

Application Example:

Jackson noticed his team had low morale and lacked cohesion and trust. Determined to improve this, he set up regular " Check-In Chats," where the sole focus was on hearing team members' thoughts, challenges, and ideas. During one of the sessions, Jackson practiced active listening by nodding, maintaining eye contact, and summarizing what was said to confirm understanding.

Example:

If I'm hearing you correctly you said that you felt the same way when taking on a project that you haven't seen in a while. Is that correct?

In other meetings, Jackson went deeper and encouraged deeper conversations by asking open-ended questions, which significantly improved team dynamics and trust.

Part 3: Sharing and Encouraging Vulnerability

This step involves leaders sharing their own vulnerabilities and encouraging team members to do the same. Sharing personal experiences and emotions helps humanize leaders and build a stronger, more connected team.

Goal: *To foster a culture of openness and mutual trust within the team.*

Exercise:

- **Share Your Own Vulnerabilities:** Start by sharing a personal story that highlights your vulnerabilities. Ensure the story is appropriate and relevant to the team.

- **Invite Team Members to Share:** Encourage team members to share their own vulnerabilities. Create a safe space where they feel comfortable doing so.

- **Provide Support and Feedback:** Offer support and constructive feedback to team members who share their vulnerabilities. Acknowledge their courage and validate their feelings.

Reflection Questions:

1. How did sharing my vulnerabilities affect my relationship with the team?

2. What challenges did I face in encouraging my team to share their vulnerabilities?

3. How can I continue to support my team in being open and vulnerable?

Application Example:

Initially hesitant to be vulnerable, Jackson learned from a past mistake where his openness was dismissed. He later found the right balance. During a team meeting, Jackson shared a personal story about a campaign that flopped spectacularly. This act of vulnerability encouraged his team members to open up about their own challenges, creating a more supportive environment.

Part 4: Reflecting and Reinforcing

This step focuses on reflecting on and reinforcing the importance of vulnerability practices within the team. Regular reflection helps ensure that the team continues to value and practice vulnerability.

Goal: *To sustain a culture of vulnerability and openness within the team.*

Exercise:

- **Schedule Regular Reflections:** Set aside time regularly to reflect on the team's progress in practicing vulnerability. Discuss what has been working and what can be improved.

- **Seek Feedback:** Ask team members for feedback about how the practice of vulnerability has impacted them and the team as a whole.

- **Reinforce Positive Behaviors:** Acknowledge and reward team members who consistently practice and encourage vulnerability.

Reflection Questions:

1. How has the practice of vulnerability changed the team dynamics?

2. What feedback have I received from the team about our vulnerability practices?

3. What steps can I take to reinforce the importance of vulnerability in the future?

Application Example:

Jackson's commitment to vulnerability was reinforced through regular reflection and feedback sessions. In a bi-weekly team meeting, he initiates a reflection session on the team's practice of vulnerability. Jackson encourages open discussion on recent experiences, such as one colleague sharing their struggle with a project deadline, and gathers anonymous feedback on the impact of these practices. Jackson acknowledges this positive behavior and emphasizes the importance of continued openness. The feedback loop further reinforced the spiritually-centered practice of vulnerability.

By creating an environment that valued openness, Jackson continuously improved team dynamics and furthered a supportive culture. His journey from an Emotionally Zipped-Up Leader *to a* Leader in Emotionally Out-there Mode strengthened his leadership style, which recharged and recalibrated his team.

GUIDE SUMMARY

My goal for this guide is to teach you how to balance vulnerability with professionalism by setting boundaries, practicing active listening, and creating a culture of mutual respect. You'll create a more open, trusting, and collaborative work environment by sharing appropriate personal insights, supporting your team, and reflecting on these practices. Embrace these steps to strengthen your leadership and enhance team dynamics, leading to greater connection and collective wins.

So, did I hit my goal?

The best way to find out if you can trust somebody is to trust them.

—ERNEST HEMINGWAY

FROM THE FRONT LINES:
REAL STORIES OF VULNERABLE LEADERS

Now that you've learned about the importance of vulnerability and how to implement it with those that you lead, let's explore real stories of leaders who achieved remarkable success by embracing vulnerability. These stories illustrate how the spiritually centered practices of openness, honesty, and empathy transform leadership and inspire positive change.

Shirley Chisholm: Champion of Vulnerable Leadership

Shirley Chisholm was a trailblazing politician who used vulnerability to connect deeply with her constituents. As the first African American woman elected to the U.S. Congress, she didn't hide the challenges she faced. Instead, she spoke openly about the myriad obstacles she faced as a Black woman in a predominantly white and male political arena. This honesty made her relatable to many who felt marginalized and unheard, allowing her to build trust and strong connections with her supporters.

Chisholm balanced her vulnerability with strength by *selectively sharing* her experiences. She didn't expose every detail of her personal life, but she was candid about the struggles she encountered. This approach showcased her resilience and authenticity, making her a powerful and effective leader. Her campaign slogan, "Unbought and Unbossed," reflected her commitment to independence and transparency, further endearing her to voters who admired her courage and integrity.

Her ability to connect on a personal level and her fearless advocacy for equality and justice left a lasting impact on American politics. Chisholm's legacy demonstrates that true leadership involves being genuine and open. It also shows that vulnerability, when balanced with strength, inspires and drives meaningful change.

John Chambers: Leading Cisco with Openness and Empathy

John Chambers, the former CEO of Cisco Systems, is another example of a leader who harnessed vulnerability to connect with his team and drive success. From 1995 to 2015, Chambers grew Cisco into a global technology giant. He was known for sharing personal stories and openly discussing his challenges, which helped him build trust and create a supportive corporate culture.

Chambers emphasized transparency and open communication, encouraging his team to share their ideas and concerns without fear. By admitting his own failures and setbacks, he created a safe environment where innovation thrived. This approach not only strengthened team cohesion but also contributed to Cisco's remarkable growth during his tenure.

Chambers' leadership style showed that vulnerability is a powerful tool for creating an inclusive and innovative workplace. His openness about personal experiences set an example, humanizing leadership and building stronger connections within the organization. This vulnerability-driven approach helped Cisco achieve significant success and established Chambers as a visionary leader in the tech industry.

These two amazing people show us that the strongest leaders are those who care deeply, are not afraid to make mistakes and treat themselves and others with kindness. They prove that you can be vulnerable and in charge while still making a huge impact.

Leadership is not about being in charge.
It is about taking care of those in your charge.

—SIMON SINEK

ZIPPING UP THE CHAPTER BUT OPENING UP TO HIGHER-LEVEL ADAPTABLE AND FLUID LEADERSHIP

I hope I've been successful in making a case for vulnerability. My point is that it isn't about giving away all of our secrets or sharing everything with everyone. It's about choosing which parts of ourselves to share generally without getting into the weeds to connect with and help others. We create a deeper connection by acknowledging how others feel, relating through our own similar experiences, and sharing what we've discovered.

It's taken me a very long time to figure out the right things to say to the right people. At times, I still say the right thing to the wrong person. And from time to time, I'll get it all wrong and say under my breath, *"Eric, what were you thinking? I went overboard and said too much. That wasn't useful in making a connection."* However, through empathy and shared experiences, I've learned to navigate these situations better, it's essential to set appropriate boundaries between personal and professional settings. The idea is to share just enough to show understanding and offer insights without overwhelming others or feeling icky inside afterward.

At one time or another, we've all had that queasy feeling in the pit of our stomachs after being open. The scenario about Jackson being vulnerable early in his career among his peers and the response that made him regret his decision is relatable to most of us. That's why many people don't do it again.

Being appropriately open in a professional setting can take some practice. It's like learning to ride a bike without training wheels—wobbly at first, but with each pedal, you gain confidence and balance. It's about taking those small risks that show others that you're a human just like them. Expressing understanding, reflecting on common experiences, and revealing helpful insights make these moments smoother and more impactful.

Imagine two colleagues under immense pressure to meet a tight deadline. One of them decides to break the silence, admitting their struggle to keep up. This moment of openness prompts the other to share their own difficulties with the project. This exchange fosters mutual understanding and support, allowing them to effectively discuss and implement strategies to manage their workload. Their shared vulnerability eases individual stress and strengthens their working relationship.

We saw how leaders like Shirley Chisholm and John Chambers used vulnerability to create trust and drive success. Shirley Chisholm, the first African American woman elected to the U.S. Congress, was known for her candidness. She didn't hide her struggles but shared them openly, which resonated with many and built a strong, supportive network around her. John Chambers, former CEO of Cisco, admitted his own mistakes and what he learned from them, turning his vulnerabilities into powerful leadership lessons.

My old boss Walter and the character Jackson show that vulnerability is courageous and a real strength. Putting yourself out there is higher-level leadership stuff. Our willingness to share our struggles and uncertainties says we're authentic, making people feel more comfortable. It takes a special kind of leader—a "Spiritually-Centered Higher-Level Leader"—to create a space where everyone feels safe in taking these risks. Higher-level leaders understand that when we all share a little bit of ourselves, we weave a strong net to catch those who fall. It's a net made of trust, care, and the belief that we're all in this together.

Imagine leading a team where everyone's unique talents shine bright, and each success adds to the group's glow. That's the beauty of interdependence. It's not about losing who you are; it's about finding out how you contribute to something bigger. Picture a scenario where a project team is struggling with a complex problem. Instead of dictating solutions, the leader admits to uncertainty and invites everyone to share their thoughts. This vulnerability sparks creativity, and soon, ideas flow freely. Each team member feels valued and essential, leading to a breakthrough that would have been impossible in a more guarded environment.

Consider a community initiative aimed at improving local parks. The project leader shares their personal connection to the parks, revealing childhood memories and hopes for future generations. This personal touch inspires volunteers to open up about their own stories, creating a sense of shared purpose and deepening commitment. The project achieves its goals and builds lasting bonds among community members.

So, as I close this chapter, remember that vulnerability is courage. We can do courageous things to make the world a better place. Embrace who you are, share it with others, and watch as the world opens up to you in return. Vulnerability in leadership isn't a sign of weakness; it's the ultimate act of strength and trust. It's the key to building teams that are not just effective but also deeply connected and resilient.

I challenge you to take a step toward being more vulnerable in your professional setting. Start by sharing a small, relatable personal story or admitting a struggle to a *trusted colleague.* Notice how this act of openness fosters a deeper connection and mutual support. By embracing vulnerability, you create a ripple effect that encourages others to do the same. Are you ready to lead at a higher level and transform your relationships? Take the first step today and watch the positive impact unfold.

Vulnerability is the essence of connection and connection is the essence of existence.

—LEO CHRISTOPHER

RESOURCES

EXPERTS ON VULNERABILITY

Navigating the complexities of our emotions and relationships is a journey that many find challenging yet essential. Having a coach to come alongside you in your journey to become a higher-level leader can be incredibly beneficial. Below are several authors on the topics of vulnerability, emotional intelligence, and seeking support. Through their extensive research and compelling writings, these thought leaders offer insights and tools to help us better understand ourselves and connect more deeply with others. From groundbreaking concepts to practical strategies, their works help to leverage our emotions and enhance our personal and professional lives.

Brené Brown is a researcher and storyteller who explores vulnerability, courage, and empathy. Her book "Daring Greatly" teaches us that embracing vulnerability can transform our lives, relationships, and work. She also wrote "Atlas of the Heart," mapping out 87 human emotions to help us better understand our feelings.

Daniel Goleman brought emotional intelligence (EI) to the mainstream with his bestseller "Emotional Intelligence: Why It Can Matter More Than IQ." His work explains how understanding and managing our emotions can improve our relationships, performance, and overall well-being.

Marc Brackett is a Yale professor and the author of "Permission to Feel." His book introduces the RULER system, which helps people recognize, understand, label, express, and regulate their emotions to lead healthier, more fulfilling lives.

Susan David's book "Emotional Agility" shows how to navigate life's twists and turns with a balance of positivity and realism. She teaches us to face our emotions head-on and adapt to change with grace and resilience.

Harriet Lerner is a psychologist known for her book The Dance of Connection. In it, she emphasizes the importance of honest conversations and emotional bravery in strengthening relationships and dealing with conflicts.

Esther Perel is a therapist and author of "The State of Affairs" and "Mating in Captivity." She explores the complexities of modern relationships, emphasizing the importance of vulnerability and emotional intelligence in maintaining intimacy and connection.

Joan Rosenberg is a psychologist who wrote "90 Seconds to a Life You Love." Her book teaches how to handle unpleasant feelings and develop emotional resilience, empowering readers to live more confidently and authentically.

By exploring their works, we open ourselves to a richer, more empathetic, and resilient existence. Whether you are seeking personal growth, better relationships, or leadership skills, these authors offer invaluable resources to support your journey.

Chapter 4:
Practice Four, Compassion

THE SPIRITUALLY CENTERED HIGHER-LEVEL VISIONARY AND EXPANSIVE LEADER

ELEMENT THREE: VISIONARY AND EXPANSIVE 🌬️

ADVANCE CLEAR COMMUNICATION AND EXPANSIVE THINKING, EMPOWERING INNOVATIVE AND FORWARD-THINKING IDEAS

During my time at the music distribution company, we were assigned a particularly complex project that had more hurdles than a track meet. We were behind schedule, and there were constant changes in requirements. When my boss, Walter, the regional sales manager, addressed his concerns and acknowledged our efforts, it was more of a relief than a discouragement. Many of us made our share of mistakes, including me, on a critical segment that I spearheaded. It was decided that I would have a talk with Walter. It went something like this.

I felt terrible. I went to Walter, my stomach in knots.

"Walter, I'm really sorry," I said, making eye contact. *"Our team messed up. Big time."*

Walter nodded knowingly. *"I know that you've put in a lot of overtime on this, Eric. Thanks for coming to see me. I've been keeping an eye on the progress, and I'm aware of the mistakes that have been happening,"* he said, his tone calm and reassuring. *"This reminds me of a project we had a few years ago. We hit a lot of bumps along the way. But through those mistakes, we found new solutions that we never would have considered otherwise."*

I looked up, surprised. *"But we really messed up,"* I insisted. *"We feel like we've let you down."*

Walter chuckled softly. *"Do you think I've never messed up? Let me tell you more about that project. We were working with a major customer, and it seemed like everything that could go wrong did go wrong. The scope of the project changed significantly, as did the requirements. I was the third person assigned to the project, the first two had been fired. The existing team lost key members. I had to scramble to find their replacements and they didn't fit in well. I underestimated the significance of the team's initial distrust of me. They believed I had gotten rid of their friends. But somehow, we made it through all the mistakes, the fractured trust, and chaos. The remarkable thing was we found innovative solutions that actually improved the final product. We learned a lot from it, making the group come together and making me a stronger leader."*

His words felt like a warm blanket on a cold day. Walter's honesty and his willingness to share his own experiences made me feel less incompetent.

"We'll figure this out together," he continued. *"Let's look at what went wrong and see how we can fix it. And more importantly, let's see what we can learn from it."*

Later, in the team meeting, Walter addressed everyone. *"I know many of you are feeling down about the recent mistakes,"* he began. *"I also know the things that are out of your control and the extra hard work that you've all been putting in to fix the issues."* Walter shared the same story with the team that he had shared with me earlier.

The team seemed to relax a bit, the tension in the room easing.

Walter continued, *"Now, let's brainstorm solutions together. I believe in each one of you, and I know we can turn this around. Let's discuss what went wrong and how we can address it."*

The team began sharing ideas, and Walter facilitated the discussion, ensuring everyone had a chance to speak.

"We need to improve our communication," one team member suggested. *"Maybe daily stand-up meetings could help us stay on the same page."*

"That's a good idea," Walter said. *"Let's implement that starting tomorrow."*

"I noticed one of our suppliers is behind on deliveries, and there are many issues with the orders." Another person added. *"Can we schedule a meeting with them to see what's going on?"*

"I'll handle that," Walter replied. *"I'll talk to them and see what kind of resolution we can come up with. They'll appreciate the phone call; we've been their long-time customer."*

Walter then turned to me. *"I'd like you to lead the effort to improve our workflow processes. Identify the bottlenecks and suggest improvements."*

I nodded, feeling a renewed sense of purpose. *"I'll get started on it right away."*

Walter closed the meeting by saying, *"I presented you all to the executive team to take on this particular project because of the strength and camaraderie of the group. Each person brings a unique and diverse set of talents, making this a dream team. I see us crushing this project, delivering something they never thought possible. When that happens, I know we'll win the regional excellence award this year. So, with that being said, I also know that you'll solve the riddles in this project and succeed in building something great."*

By the end of the meeting, we had a clear plan, new assignments, and renewed energy. The atmosphere was electrified, and everyone seemed ready to tackle the challenges ahead.

Walter's Wisdom: Turning Blunders into Bonds

Walter shared his story about a past project and the lessons learned, both good and bad. He was open and real, sharing just enough details to help us understand without going too deep. His honesty and acknowledgment reinvigorated the team, including me, and brought us closer together, making us determined to succeed in completing the project.

I also saw the humanity side of leadership with Walter. By revealing past experiences and what he did to move ahead, Walter made it safe for the team to continue being upfront when challenges popped up. This created an atmosphere where learning and growing were more important than blaming. His approach showed that facing mistakes directly leads to new ideas and a stronger bond. This openness helped us seize the opportunity to leverage our mistakes to get better.

Walter's compassion throughout the project was key. He treated each person with understanding and patience, highlighting the importance of second chances. This enabled us to dust ourselves off and problem-solve. His ability to connect with the team on a personal level reinforced that leadership isn't just about giving orders but also about rolling up your sleeves and helping out.

Thanks to Walter's expressed vision, the team became unified and motivated once again. We felt more responsible for our roles and eager to do our part to make the project a success. The trust and appreciation Walter showed that day led to deeper relationships and a higher level of respect. My big takeaway was the value of being open at work, the importance of understanding other people, and then jumping in to support them.

Embracing a spiritually-centered approach means looking at the bigger picture and understanding how we impact the world around us. It's about aligning our goals with a higher purpose and making decisions that reflect our core values. This visionary leadership style encourages us to explore new possibilities, challenge the status quo, and have a future where we can find common ground to make a meaningful difference.

Forward-thinking ideas thrive in an environment where openness and compassion are celebrated. When leaders are willing to share their own challenges and what they've learned from them, it sets the stage for others to do the same. This openness leads to an innovative environment where everyone is empowered to contribute their best ideas.

Ultimately, the experience reinforced that higher-level leadership is about inspiring others through tough times with a combination of transparency, honesty, compassion, and a spiritually-centered vision.

Compassion and tolerance are not a
sign of weakness but a sign of strength.

—DALAI LAMA

COMPASSION IN ACTION: EMMA'S BLUNDER IS SARAH'S BREAKTHROUGH

Emma, the project manager, was sitting in her office after the team meeting with Jackson. The meeting was a training on how to be appropriately vulnerable at work. Jackson demonstrated workplace vulnerability by opening up about his feeling of being an imposter dressed up as a leader. His sharing made her realize that she wasn't alone in feeling the same way, which renewed her sense of belonging. Just then, there was a knock at the door.

"Come in!" Emma called out, Turning around in her chair.

The door opened, and Sarah, the new hire, stepped in. She looked visibly upset, her eyes slightly red, as if she had been holding back tears.

"Hey, Sarah. Everything okay?" Emma asked, her voice gentle yet curious.

"Not really," Sarah admitted, her voice filled with frustration. *"I just made a huge mistake on the project, but it's not my fault. The instructions that Jackson gave me were so unclear."*

Emma motioned for Sarah to take a seat. *"I know that feeling all too well,"* she said, a warm smile spreading across her face. *"Can I tell you something?"*

Sarah sat down, looking both nervous and intrigued, and said, *"Sure, I guess Emma."*

"Just recently, I was working on a major project with a very tight deadline," Emma began. *"I was so focused on getting everything just right that I overlooked a crucial detail in the final report. When Jackson pointed it out, I felt like the ground had opened up beneath me. I thought I had failed, and honestly, I felt completely inadequate. I realized later that I didn't ask the right questions. Had I gotten clarification, the whole thing probably never would've happened."*

Sarah's eyes widened in surprise. *"Really? You can't possibly always ask the right questions. I've only heard great things about you."*

Emma laughed softly. *"Thank you, but believe me, I have my moments. In fact, just today, Jackson shared in our meeting that he sometimes feels like he has imposter syndrome, too. It was a powerful reminder that we're all human and we all make mistakes."*

Sarah's expression softened. *"So, how did you deal with it?"*

"Well, after I got over the initial shock, I decided to own up to my mistake," Emma said. *"I apologized to the team, and we all worked together to fix the issues in the report. It wasn't easy, but it taught me that it's okay to be vulnerable and admit when you've messed up. It actually brought us closer as a team."*

Sarah looked thoughtful for a moment but then shrugged. *"I guess, but in my case, it really wasn't my fault. The system crashed, and the instructions were so unclear. How am I supposed to work with that?"*

Emma leaned forward, her tone becoming more encouraging. *"I understand that sometimes things are out of our control, but ...can I tell you something?*

Sarah perked up with nervous enthusiasm, *"Sure."*

Emma continued, *"Taking responsibility for our part in the situation is important. Blaming external factors can prevent us from learning and growing."*

In deep thought, Sarah put her head down.

Emma paused for a moment, then smiled warmly at Sarah. *"You know what? Let's take a break. How about we go grab some lunch and talk this through? My treat."*

Sarah looked surprised but grateful. *"Really? You'd do that?"*

"Of course," Emma replied with a reassuring smile. *"I need to get away from my desk, and a nice walk to lunch with a new friend would be good for both of us."*

They headed to a nearby café, where Emma ordered their lunches and found a cozy corner to sit in. Emma listened attentively for the next thirty minutes as Sarah vented her frustrations. Emma shared more of her own experiences of making mistakes and feeling inadequate, which created a safe space for Sarah to express herself.

"Thank you for this, Emma," Sarah said, her voice filled with gratitude. *"It means a lot to me that you took the time to listen and share your own stories."*

Emma reached across the table and gave Sarah's hand a gentle squeeze. *"Anytime, Sarah. What matters is what we do when we misstep. Taking responsibility for our actions, even when things go wrong, is key to growth."*

As Sarah and Emma walked back to the office, Emma thought to herself how far she had come in improving her attitude and how making better connections was putting a smile on her face more often.

Emma suggested they spend a few more minutes at the office reviewing the project details. They brainstormed solutions, working collaboratively to improve the process overall. Sarah's confidence visibly grew as they worked together.

"Thank you so much, Emma," Sarah said as they wrapped up. *"I feel so much better now."*

Emma placed a hand on Sarah's shoulder. *"Anytime, Sarah. Next time, don't be afraid to ask questions before doing something you're not sure about."*

As Sarah left the office with a renewed purpose, Emma felt a deep sense of fulfillment. Instead of dismissing Sarah's feelings, she had taken action to help a colleague in need. This experience reaffirmed her belief in the power of compassion in action.

Rewind to When Emma Wasn't Quite the Beacon of Inspiration

After yet another long week of late nights and endless cups of coffee, Emma felt a knot in her stomach. She had poured everything into the project, yet she couldn't shake the feeling that she had let Jackson down when the deadline came. Emma's boss had placed his trust in her, and despite valiant efforts, she feared her performance hadn't hit her own impossibly high standards. The weight of self-criticism and disappointment was almost unbearable, and she found herself spiraling into a familiar cycle of harsh self-judgment and off-the-chart anxiety.

Jackson, who had his own struggles with imposter syndrome, discovered the power of vulnerability and mindfulness, and his openness sparked Emma's interest in changing. She had always been a perfectionist with sky-high expectations of herself, but getting on the path to mindfulness began to soften her inner dialogue.

Emma started her days with mindfulness practice, carving out time to center herself before diving into her daily responsibilities. This simple shift had quite an effect on her attitude. She was less critical of her imperfections and more appreciative of her efforts. It was as if a new lightness had entered her demeanor, with energy soaring.

Emma's journey didn't stop with mindfulness. At first, being compassionate with herself felt foreign—almost counterintuitive— offering herself kindness when she felt she deserved criticism. But slowly, Emma began to understand that treating herself with the same empathy she would extend to a friend was not only healing but transformative. Emma started by acknowledging her feelings without judgment, recognizing that it was okay to feel disappointed and frustrated after doing her best. Instead of chastising herself, Emma offered words of comfort and encouragement, reminding herself that everyone makes mistakes.

The impact of these practices was profound. Emma's brain seemed to relax as the stress hormones gave way to a surge of feel-good chemicals. The incessant chatter of self-doubt quieted, replaced by a sense of calm and security. This inner shift didn't just make her feel better—it fundamentally changed how she approached her work and interactions. She became more patient and understanding.

Emma began to see setbacks as opportunities for growth rather than definitive failures. This new mindset helped her become a support system for those around her. One person who particularly benefited from Emma's new approach was her colleague Sarah. Sarah had been struggling to learn her new job and the inevitable mistakes that come with it. Emma could listen without judgment, provide comfort, and share her own experiences.

Looking back, Emma finally realized that feeling like she had let Jackson down was the catalyst for a transformation. It pushed her to explore self-compassion, to embrace imperfections, and to grow from experiences. Emma's journey with mindfulness and self-compassion served as a powerful reminder that inner work is not just a personal endeavor—it's a pathway to better connect with and uplift those around us. In learning to be kind to herself, she discovered a wellspring of strength and empathy that enriched both her personal and professional life. Emma was stepping further and further away from perfectionism and running to the standard of excellence.

GUIDE TO SELF-COMPASSION

Part A: Practicing Kindness and Understanding Toward Yourself

This guide was inspired by Dr. Kristin Neff's work and is a mindfulness-based exercise designed to help us pause during difficult moments and treat ourselves with kindness and understanding. It involves acknowledging our suffering, recognizing that suffering is part of the human experience, and offering ourselves compassion. Complementing this with Part B: Loving-Kindness Meditation further enhances feelings of compassion toward ourselves and others.

Goal: This guide aims to help us develop self-compassion by encouraging mindfulness, recognizing shared humanity, and practicing self-kindness. This exercise is intended to help us respond to our own suffering with care and support, rather than self-criticism, while also experiencing feelings of love and kindness toward ourselves and others.

All the upcoming exercises will be based on the same Example Application Scenario: You made a mistake at work and are now feeling overwhelmed and self-critical. These exercises are designed to help you approach the situation with more kindness and self-support, guiding you to be gentler with yourself as you navigate through this challenge.

Exercise

Step 1: Acknowledge Your Struggle

Reflect on a difficult situation, thought, or emotion that is causing you distress.

Activity

Take a few moments to bring to mind a specific challenging situation. Notice how it makes you feel. Use phrases like *"This is a moment of suffering"* or *"This hurts."*

Example Application:

Scenario: You made a mistake at work and are feeling overwhelmed and self-critical.

Reflective Questions:

1. How does this situation make me feel physically and emotionally?

2. Can I name the emotions I am experiencing right now?

3. How does acknowledging my suffering help in managing my emotions?

4. What changes when I accept my pain instead of resisting it?

Answer: I am feeling really stressed and disappointed about the mistake I made.

Emma's Experience:

Scenario: Emma made a crucial error in a major project and felt overwhelmed and like an imposter.

She acknowledged her struggle by taking a moment to reflect on the situation and her feelings. She said to herself, *"This is a moment of suffering. This hurts."* This acknowledgment helped Emma name her emotions and manage her response. She realized that accepting her pain rather than resisting it allowed her to take responsibility, apologize, and work with her team to correct the mistake. She also reminded herself not to judge herself harshly, as perfection is unattainable.

Step 2: Recognize Shared Humanity

Understand that suffering is a universal experience and that you are not alone in your struggles.

Activity:

Remind yourself that everyone experiences difficulties and suffering. Use phrases like *"Suffering is a part of life"* or *"Other people feel this way too."*

Example Application:

Scenario: You made a mistake at work and are feeling overwhelmed and self-critical.

Reflective Questions:

1. How might others experience similar struggles to mine?

2. What does it mean to recognize that suffering is a part of being human?

3. How does acknowledging shared humanity change my perspective on my situation?

4. In what ways does understanding shared humanity provide comfort?

5. How can I remind myself of this connection during future challenges?

Answer: It's normal to make mistakes; everyone makes them.

Emma's Experience:

Scenario: Emma made a crucial error in a major project and felt overwhelmed and like an imposter.

She reminded herself that suffering is a part of life and that everyone makes mistakes. She thought, *"Other people feel this way too."* Recognizing that her struggles were part of the shared human experience helped Emma feel less isolated and more connected to her team. This perspective allowed her to reach out for support, understanding that she was not alone in her challenges.

Step 3: Offer Yourself Kindness

Extend compassion and kindness to yourself in the same way you would to a friend.

Activity:

Place a hand over your heart or use another soothing gesture. Say phrases like *"May I be kind to myself"* or *"May I give myself the compassion that I need."*

Example Application:

Scenario: You made a mistake at work and are feeling overwhelmed and self-critical.

Reflective Questions:

1. What words of kindness can I offer myself right now?

2. How would I treat a close friend who was experiencing the same situation?

3. What do I need to hear or feel to comfort myself in this moment?

4. What specific actions or words can I use to be kinder to myself?

5. How can self-kindness change my approach to personal challenges?

Answer: I will be patient with myself. I will learn from this experience without being harsh.

Emma's Experience:

Scenario: Emma made a crucial error in a major project and felt overwhelmed and like an imposter.

She placed a hand over her heart and said to herself, *"May I be kind to myself."* She thought about how she would support a friend in the same situation and extend that same compassion to herself. Emma reminded herself that she could learn from this experience without being harsh, allowing herself to feel more at peace and ready to move forward. By offering herself kindness, Emma was able to approach her mistake with a more compassionate and constructive mindset.

Part B: Loving-Kindness Meditation

This meditation practice involves directing positive and loving thoughts toward yourself and then extending those feelings to others. This enhances the overall practice of self-compassion by creating a sense of love and kindness.

1. Find a quiet and comfortable spot to sit or lie down.

2. Close your eyes and take a few slow, deep breaths.

3. Set an intention for your meditation, such as cultivating self-compassion or releasing stress.

4. Begin by repeating phrases like *"May I be happy," "May I be kind and gentle with myself,"* or *"May I be at peace."*

5. After generating feelings of loving-kindness toward yourself, gradually extend these feelings to others by visualizing loved ones and repeating similar phrases directed toward them.

Reflective Questions:

1. How do I feel after directing loving-kindness toward myself?

2. What changes do I notice when I extend these feelings toward others?

3. How can this practice enhance my overall sense of compassion?

4. How does practicing loving-kindness toward myself and others affect my emotional state?

5. What insights have I gained from doing this meditation?

6. How can I integrate loving-kindness meditation into my daily life?

Practicing Loving-Kindness Meditation can vary in duration based on your schedule and experience level. As a beginner, you might start with just 5 to 10 minutes per session, gradually increasing to 20 or 30 minutes as you become more comfortable. Consistency is key, so aim to practice daily or several times a week to experience the full benefits.

Example Application:

Scenario: You made a mistake at work and are feeling overwhelmed and self-critical.

I will be kind and gentle with myself as I navigate this challenge.

Example with Emma:

Scenario: Emma made a crucial error in a major project and felt overwhelmed and like an imposter.

She found a quiet spot in her office, closed her eyes, and took a few deep breaths. She set an intention to cultivate self-compassion and began her Loving-Kindness Meditation by repeating, *"May I be kind and gentle with myself."* She felt a wave of calm wash over her. After a few minutes, she extended these feelings of loving-kindness toward her colleagues, visualizing them and saying, *"May they be happy, may they be at peace."* This practice helped Emma feel more connected and compassionate toward herself and others, easing her emotional distress and improving her overall well-being.

By regularly practicing the Self-Compassion Break and Loving-Kindness Meditation, you will develop a more compassionate and supportive relationship with yourself.

The growth and development of people
is the highest calling of leadership.

—HARVEY S. FIRESTONE

FROM PERFECTIONIST TO COMPASSIONATE CRUSADER

Being self-aware, admitting there is a problem, and then working on the problem is higher-level stuff. Pain nudged Emma to look inward to identify and overcome her perfectionism. Isn't that true for all of us? Why would we change anything if it wasn't too painful to remain the same? Emma got on a new pathway and started practicing mindfulness because she wanted something healthier for herself. It didn't happen overnight, but she moved away from perfectionist activities that led to high levels of self-imposed anxiety.

One of the first practices she embraced was the Loving-Kindness Meditation. Initially, it felt awkward and forced to repeat phrases like *"May I be kind to myself"* and *"May I be at peace."* However, with consistent practice, Emma began to feel a shift. She noticed a reduction in her anxiety levels and a newfound ability to handle stress more effectively.

Being kind to herself led her to be kind to others, including Sarah. This act of compassion helped Sarah feel supported and also strengthened their working relationship. Emma's new mindset permeated into all areas of her life. She started volunteering at a local shelter, finding joy in helping others and seeing the world from different perspectives. This experience deepened her understanding of shared humanity and the struggles that everyone faces.

In her personal life, Emma made an effort to be more patient and understanding with her family and friends. For instance, when her sister vented about a bad day at work, Emma listened without interrupting or offering unsolicited advice. She realized that sometimes, people just need to be heard and validated. This new approach brought them closer, and her sister often remarked on how much she appreciated Emma's support.

Emma also began setting realistic goals for herself and her team, understanding that perfection was an unattainable standard. She encouraged her team to strive for excellence but also to embrace mistakes as learning opportunities.

Through her journey, Emma discovered that self-compassion was not just about feeling good in the moment but was a powerful tool for long-term resilience and well-being. By being kind to herself, she could be more present and compassionate with others.

BE THE ACTION:
FUN AND HEARTFELT WAYS TO CULTIVATE COMPASSION

This guide is designed to help you develop a deeper sense of empathy and compassion through practical, enjoyable exercises. It's easy to get caught up in our own lives and forget the impact we have on those around us. This guide aims to remind you of the importance of kindness and understanding. By actively practicing these spiritually centered practices, you'll improve your relationships and create a more supportive community that's a little brighter for everyone.

Goal: *To develop a deeper sense of empathy and compassion toward others, improving interpersonal relationships.*

Exercise 1: Random Acts of Kindness

Activity:

1. Identify small, thoughtful actions you can take to brighten someone's day.

2. These actions can be as simple as offering a sincere compliment, helping someone with their tasks, or surprising a colleague with their favorite beverage.

3. Perform these acts without expecting anything in return, focusing on the joy and positivity they bring to others.

Example Application:

Scenario: You notice a coworker who seems down lately.

"I will perform a random act of kindness by leaving a positive note on their desk or surprising them with their favorite snack."

Example of Emma:

Emma noticed that Sarah seemed down and stressed about work. Emma decided to perform a random act of kindness by leaving a note of encouragement and a small chocolate on Sarah's desk. This thoughtful gesture lifted Sarah's spirits and made her feel appreciated.

Exercise 2: Practicing Gratitude

Activity:

1. Each day, take a few minutes to reflect on and write down things you're grateful for about the people in your life.

2. Focus on specific actions or qualities of others that you appreciate.

3. Share your gratitude with them through a note, a message, or a conversation, expressing your appreciation sincerely.

Example Application:

Scenario: You appreciate how your friend always listens to you.

"I will practice gratitude by writing a heartfelt note to my friend, expressing how much I value their support and attentive listening."

Example of Emma:

Emma started a habit of writing gratitude notes to her team members. One day, she wrote a note to Jackson, thanking him for his vulnerability during meetings and how it inspired her. Sharing her gratitude made Jackson feel valued and motivated him to continue having an open and supportive environment.

Exercise 3: Volunteering with Diverse Groups

Activity:

1. Find a volunteering opportunity that involves working with a group of people from a different cultural or socio-economic background.

2. Approach the experience with an open mind and a willingness to learn about their perspectives and experiences.

3. Engage in conversations, participate in their activities, and offer your help and support wherever needed.

Example Application:

Scenario: You want to broaden your understanding and compassion for others.

"I will volunteer at a local community center that supports refugees, helping with language classes and participating in cultural exchange activities."

Example of Emma:

Emma decided to volunteer at a local community center that supports immigrant families. She helped with language classes and participated in cultural exchange activities. Through this experience, Emma learned about the challenges these families faced and developed a deeper sense of empathy for people with different backgrounds. This enriched her perspective and inspired her to be more inclusive in her everyday interactions.

Congratulations!

You've just taken the first steps in becoming a more compassionate individual! By embracing these fun and heartfelt exercises, you've started a journey that not only benefits those around you but also enriches your own life. Remember, compassion is a powerful force that grows stronger with practice. Continue to *"be the action"* in your daily life and watch as your efforts create ripples of kindness and understanding in your community. Keep up the great work and enjoy the profound connections you'll build along the way!

VISIONARY VOICE:
PORTRAITS OF COMPASSION IN LEADERSHIP

When you picture leaders of successful companies, do you think of them as compassionate people? It might not be the first thing that comes to mind, but that's exactly what sets spiritually-centered, high-level leaders apart from others.

Bill George is renowned not just for his leadership acumen but also for his profound sense of compassion. As the former CEO of Medtronic, a global producer of medical devices and therapies, and a Harvard Business School professor, he has consistently emphasized the importance of leading with empathy and authenticity. George believes that true leadership emerges from understanding and addressing the needs of others rather than focusing solely on personal success.

His concept of authentic leadership is deeply intertwined with emotional intelligence and mindfulness. George practices mindfulness meditation, which he credits with enhancing his self-awareness and compassion. This practice enables him to remain calm under pressure and approach leadership with a clear, compassionate mindset. He advocates for leaders to integrate their head (IQ) with their heart (EQ), believing that compassion and emotional intelligence are crucial for higher-level leadership.

George's approach to leadership is rooted in his personal experiences and challenges. The tragic losses of his mother and fiancée profoundly impacted his perspective, steering him toward a career focused on helping others through Medtronic's mission of saving lives. His teachings and writings, including books like **True North** and **Authentic Leadership,** highlight the transformative power of compassion in leadership.

George influenced countless leaders to adopt a more empathetic and supportive approach, ultimately creating more effective and humane organizational environments.

HOW COMPASSION CAN CHANGE THE WORLD

Fear of Compassion and *Perfectionism* can trap us in a relentless cycle of self-hatred. Lately, I've been seeing a great deal of what I perceive to be self-hatred in people. The cause of self-hatred is complex and isn't as simple as *just* these indicators. In this book, I focus on how non-inclusive and capitalistic-focused societies and harsh inner talk impact how we see and treat ourselves and, ultimately, how we perceive and treat others, especially those who are different from us. I'll start with the *Fear of Compassion*.

Fear of Compassion toward outgroups (social groups that a person does not identify with) stems from the belief it undermines ingroup (social groups that a person does identify with) cohesion. Dehumanizing others justifies unfair treatment and removes empathy. Discrimination arises from strong ingroup vs. outgroup dynamics, where individuals feel loyalty to their group and see others as threats. Being discriminated against can lead to self-hatred. For example, Anti-Asian sentiment and hate crimes leave many Asian Americans feeling targeted, diminishing self-worth and leading to self-hatred. Islamophobia in the U.S. linking Muslims to terrorists can lead to internalized racism and self-hatred.

The recent increase in anxiety and depression among teenagers can be linked to the toxic environment of comparison, which evolves into self-hatred. Constantly faced with the pressures of social media, academic demands, and parental expectations, teens are especially vulnerable to an environment that produces low self-esteem.

Perfectionism is the other category linked to self-hatred. I believe this is true because society pressures us to meet impossible standards of beauty and success. For instance, the rise in social media influencers who promote an unattainable lifestyle leaves many feeling inadequate.

As we've seen in the examples, Emma, like many others, struggled with perfectionism. Fueled by societal pressures, her drive for perfection kept her inner critic on overdrive. Falling short of these unrealistic standards left her feeling inadequate and self-loathing when she failed at something. Emma's journey mirrored mine, but the cause of my lack of self-compassion was much more complex. I remember my own battles with these feelings. The more I tried to achieve perfection, the more distant I felt from being kind to myself.

I've learned that our shortcomings don't define us; our ability to rise above them does. Embracing self-compassion allows us to reclaim our power. But there has to be a mechanism that activates us to claim that power. For most of us, it's pain. My health issues, stress related to work, and fast-paced, gotta-be-first-to-finish lifestyle, leading to skyrocketing anxiety, were my propellants. Practicing mindfulness was the first step in de-escalation, making significant changes in me, as was also the case for Emma.

Self-compassion was something that I thought weak people used to give themselves an excuse for failing at something. Studies of successful people like Bill George who practice mindfulness started my shift in perception. I began practicing mindfulness, and gaining self-compassion was the byproduct. It occurred to me that self-compassion doesn't make us weak. In fact, it's our superpower. Recognizing that we have flaws and understanding that others do as well breaks us free from the chains of perfectionism.

When we practice self-compassion, we start to see everyone in a new light. By being kind and patient with ourselves, we get better at understanding and being compassionate with others. Once we realize we're all imperfect and doing our best, it becomes easier to humanize the struggles of people and even those who are very different than us. We have seen what dehumanization can result in, which was the case of the genocide of World War II. Looking at people with a new set of lenses makes the possibility of offering a helping hand become much more probable.

When leaders show vulnerability and compassion, it's like throwing a pebble—the ripple effect spreads throughout their pond. By sharing their own challenges, showing they care, and claiming they "are the action," they set the pace for everyone else. This kind of higher-level leadership makes people feel worthy, and their contributions matter. Individuals are then inspired to "be the action," making their own ripple effect.

This mindset, my friend, has the potential to make a real impact. Allied, we can "be the action" and change the world for the better.

Hate is self-destructive. If you hate somebody,
you're not hurting the person you hate.
You're hurting yourself. And that's a healing.
Actually, it's a real healing, forgiveness.

—LOUIS ZAMPERINI

RESOURCES

BOOKS, STUDIES, AND ORGANIZATIONS FOR ENRICHED LEADERSHIP

Understanding the complexities of our emotions and relationships is a challenging yet essential journey. To gain deeper insights into your own ability to empathize, scan the QR code to get your empathy score. Discover how well you connect with others and uncover opportunities to enhance your emotional intelligence. Alongside your score, explore resources from renowned authors and experts who delve into compassion, providing tools and insights to help you strengthen your connections and enrich both your personal and professional life.

bit.ly/getyourempathyscore

- *The Art of Happiness* by Dalai Lama and Howard Cutler – This book provides insights into the mind of the Dalai Lama and his views on sources of happiness, including compassion.

- *Self-Compassion: The Proven Power of Being Kind to Yourself* by Kristin Neff. Kristin Neff is a leading researcher on self-compassion, and her work offers practical advice on cultivating compassion toward oneself.

- *Altruism: The Power of Compassion to Change Yourself and the World* by Matthieu Ricard – A book by a Buddhist monk who has participated in scientific studies about how meditation affects the brain, particularly in areas related to compassion.

RESEARCH STUDIES AND ACADEMIC JOURNALS

- Empirical studies in psychology journals such as the *Journal of Personality and Social Psychology* often publish research related to empathy, compassion, and altruism.

- Mindfulness research, including studies by **Jon Kabat-Zinn** and others who have explored how mindfulness meditation can foster compassion.

- Research Finding by **Harvard Business Review**: A Harvard Business Review study delves into the nuances of compassionate leadership, identifying it as a multifaceted approach that significantly benefits both the professional and personal aspects of an employee's life. The study outlines the four critical components of compassionate leadership: noticing others' needs, understanding their challenges, empathizing, and taking steps to alleviate distress. The impact of such leadership extends beyond immediate work satisfaction, potentially improving family dynamics and the personal relationships of employees. This suggests that leaders who adopt and foster compassion can create a workplace that supports their team's overall well-being, leading to happier and more productive employees. Readers interested in these findings can learn more at the Harvard Business Review's official website or specific publications on the subject (Harvard Business Publishing).

ORGANIZATIONS

- **The Greater Good Science Center at UC Berkeley**—This organization offers many resources, including articles and courses on the science of a meaningful life, which focuses heavily on compassion.

- **The Center for Compassion and Altruism Research and Education** (CCARE) at Stanford University conducts research on compassion and altruistic behavior, often publishing its findings and offering public education.

Chapter 5:
Practice Five, Forgiving

THE SPIRITUALLY CENTERED HIGHER-LEVEL VISIONARY AND EXPANSIVE LEADER

ELEMENT THREE: VISIONARY AND EXPANSIVE 🌬️

ADVANCE CLEAR COMMUNICATION AND EXPANSIVE THINKING, EMPOWERING INNOVATIVE AND FORWARD-THINKING IDEAS

In the previous chapter, we explored compassion and how understanding another person's feelings helps us "be the action" in helping them. Walter showed compassion to me and the team by getting a clear understanding of what went wrong so we could use those mistakes as lessons to move forward with a new plan. I agreed to accept the assignment of uncovering any workflow issues and finding out if there were any bottlenecks. Here's what happened next.

As I walked into Walter's office, he was pacing the room, his stride brisk and his face set in a serious expression.

Hey Walter, you wanted to see me? I asked.

"Come in, come in, and take a seat, Eric, I need to talk to you about something," Walter said. His demeanor was composed, but he looked tense.

I nervously sat down across from him; I could feel something was wrong. Walter was normally quite at ease.

With a controlled but stern voice, Walter broke the silence and said, *"I hear you had it out with your helpmate the other day."*

"Yes, I did, but he deserved it, he really made us all look bad," I said.

Walter took his glasses off and paused, then said, *"I understand why you were upset, but let's talk about how we can handle these situations better in the future."*

I shifted slightly in my seat. *"I know, but it was a huge mistake. How can I trust him again?"*

Walter nodded, acknowledging the gravity of the situation. *"Trust is important, and it can be rebuilt. Way back, I worked with a guy who I thought was a real screw-up. I'll just call him Henry for the sake of this story. Henry made a lot of mistakes, and the rest of the team had to pick up the slack. I got madder and madder, and resentments built up day by day. The team covered up for him because he was the boss's son-in-law, and we didn't think the boss would believe us if we told him we were covering for him."*

I looked inquisitively and asked. *"What happened?"*

Walter leaned back, his tone calm. *"My confidant told me that everyone makes mistakes, and how we handle them defines our humanity. Instead of focusing on the mistakes, he encouraged me to understand why Henry was making them. I had coffee with Henry, listened to his side, and talked about why he was having so many problems. As it turns out, he felt like no one on the team liked him because he was the boss's son-in-law and didn't earn his spot. He was making mistakes because he wanted to get fired and get another job. I wanted to help the guy. So, we met with the rest of the boys and worked things out. After that, Henry became a valuable member of the team. This act of getting to know him led me to give him a break. We resolved the issues and also built trust between all of us and a tight bond that has lasted to this day."*

I sighed, *"I see your point. But staying calm in the moment is tough."*

Walter smiled warmly. *"It is, but it's a skill you can develop. When you feel your temperature rising, take a deep breath and remind yourself that we're all human. Approach the situation with the mindset that these are opportunities to "be the action" in tolerating others.*

I nodded slowly, absorbing Walter's words. *"I really need to think about giving him another chance."*

Walter's smile broadened. *"That's a great start. I think deep down, you know that giving him a break is higher-level stuff, especially when he stumbles and makes you look bad. Forgiving him will show a higher standard of behavior and maybe you'll even make a new friend. You know, we don't always know what people are going through. I prejudged Henry and thought he was a real screw-up, but I was wrong about him. His mistakes weren't the definition of who he really was.*

I stood up, feeling a mix of relief and uneasiness. *"Thanks, Walter. I appreciate the talk."*

Walter clapped me on the shoulder. *"I'm always here to help. You've got this. Keep focusing on being the action and setting the standard."*

As I left the office, I felt that I needed to absorb what Walter was saying to me. This seemed like important stuff, and I needed to consider my next move seriously.

Forgive others, not because they deserve forgiveness, but because you deserve peace.

—JONATHAN HUIE

LETTING GO:
THE LEADERSHIP POWER-UP I DIDN'T KNOW THAT I NEEDED

As with many of my conversations with Walter, it was easy to open up about why I lost my cool with my helpmate. He made a big mistake that I felt reflected on me. Miguel Ruiz, the author of the book *The Four Agreements,* talks about not taking things personally in agreement number two. The actions of others aren't about me or my worth. My responses to situations have a hand in my self-worth, and those are under my control. But what would I do with that power?

I thought about how I might hold my helpmate's mistake over him for a little while longer. In the past, I kind of liked withholding forgiveness from people who hurt me. It was a weird sort of revenge that gave me a rush. But I was starting to see that I was actually giving the other person my power. Would they continue to disturb my tranquility? Was it, in fact, harming my physical and mental health to hold on to grudges?

Walter, always the wise and experienced mentor, shared the story that opened my eyes to the secrets of forgiveness. Doing a double take was difficult for him because it meant he might have made a mistake in pre-judging his co-worker. It also meant that he was no longer letting the power of resentment hang over him.

Instead of focusing on the mistake, he decided to understand why the missteps were happening. This helped him change his emotional state from angry to centered and created a chance to fix the issue and reconcile with Henry, the "screw-up."

I started thinking about the people from my past who I could never ask—or even want to ask—why they hurt or offended me. While I may never know why they acted that way, I still have control over how I choose to respond.

I considered why my helpmate missed that critical deadline, which made me look bad. It was easy to assume he was careless or lazy. But he might have been dealing with personal issues, like a sick family member or relationship trouble. His mistake might have been due to incompetence, but maybe it was a heavy heart that divided his attention.

I also thought about a family member who had snapped at me during a conversation. I felt hurt and confused by their outburst. Maybe they were struggling with financial stress at the time, and I mistakenly triggered them. Their frustration wasn't about me; it was about the pressures they were under.

I thought about a particular politician who made a controversial statement about a decision they made. I immediately judged them harshly. I never considered that they might be privy to confidential information or dealing with intense political pressure. Their actions might be influenced by factors I was unaware of, making decisions more complex.

Forgiveness isn't about overlooking the wrong or pretending it didn't happen—it's about choosing to rise above it. Nelson Mandela's saying, *"Not forgiving someone is like drinking poison and expecting the other person to die,"* is a strong way to say that by refusing to forgive, we carry an emotional burden that ultimately harms us more than the person who caused the offense. The choice to forgive frees us to move ahead with a clear mind and an unburdened heart.

I then asked myself the question, was it really about another person or was it something in me that needed to be forgiven? My awakening to the power of forgiveness reshaped the way I perceived events and the way I imagined they should be. It involved deep personal reflection and the courage to address resentments that had formed over time. I also came to believe that I had a part in these events, and it required me to deal with and then forgive myself for past behaviors and missteps.

This internal shift was profound. It stripped away the layers of shame and self-criticism that weighed me down. As I let go of my own baggage, I found it easier to give others a break and tolerate their humanness. I realized holding onto anger was pointless.

Imagine forgiveness as a river that carries away the heavy stones of anger and resentment. When we choose to let go, we allow the current to cleanse us, making room for new growth and understanding. Forgiveness is so important—it frees us from past hurts. We might not know the full story behind a person's mistake; they could be overwhelmed, distracted, or simply human. It's in those moments that our higher-level qualities shine through.

Reflecting on Walter's wisdom, I decided to apologize to my helpmate and give him another chance. Forgiving him wasn't just about letting go of my resentments; it showed that I trusted him with a chance to learn and grow. When I was able to release my taste for savoring the power of withholding forgiveness, I knew it was higher-level stuff.

I have to admit that forgiving is a never-ending process. Doing it improves our well-being including good physical and mental health. And it helps us to build stronger connections. Connecting with others at a deeper level is where happiness resides.

Forgiveness is not an occasional act;
it is a constant attitude.

—MARTIN LUTHER KING JR.

COMMUNICATION GAP: SARAH AND JACKSON'S FALLOUT

Sarah, the new hire, was on the phone with her mother after she and her project manager, Emma, finished up their brainstorming session. Sarah was complaining to her mother that her boss, Jackson, hadn't given her clear instructions and that it was his fault she made so many mistakes. Just then, he walked up behind her.

As Jackson approached Sarah's desk, he overheard her complaint. Despite his mindfulness practices and his personal growth, the words stung. He took a deep breath, trying to steady himself and remind himself to respond thoughtfully.

"Hey Sarah, can we talk for a minute?" Jackson said, unable to keep the edge out of his voice this time.

Sarah quickly said goodbye to her mother and hung up, looking slightly startled. *"Oh, hi, Jackson. Sure, what's up?"*

Jackson's irritation was bubbling just beneath the surface. *"I overheard a bit of your conversation. I had no idea you had questions about the tasks I assigned."*

Sarah looked down, fidgeting with her pen. *"I didn't want to bother you. I thought I should figure it out on my own."*

Jackson's frustration broke through. *"Figure it out on your own? Really, Sarah? Those mistakes happened because you didn't ask for help. You need to communicate if you're unsure about something."*

Sarah nodded, her face reddening. *"I'm sorry. I just didn't want to look like an idiot."*

Jackson's patience was wearing thin. *"Everyone has questions, especially when they're new. It's part of the learning process. What's upsetting is that you felt you couldn't come to me."*

Sarah looked up, feeling defensive and somewhat flippant. *"Well, maybe if your instructions were clearer, I wouldn't have to ask so many questions."*

Jackson was taken aback by her tone. He tried to take a deep breath, but his annoyance was hard to suppress. *"My instructions are clear, Sarah. It's your responsibility to ask for clarification if you don't understand something."*

Sarah shrugged, looking away. *"I asked Emma for help, and she was great."*

Jackson forced a smile, but it didn't reach his eyes. *"I'm looking forward to getting the corrected report once you're finished."*

Without waiting for a response, Jackson turned and walked away, leaving Sarah at her desk, feeling a mix of relief and apprehension. She couldn't help but feel guilty for her tone and frustrated that Jackson didn't seem to understand her perspective.

Mindfulness vs. Office Drama

In the chat between Jackson and Sarah, it's clear both of them could have handled things better. Jackson overheard Sarah complaining about his instructions, and despite his mindfulness training and personal growth, it really got under his skin. He tried to keep his cool at first, but his irritation started to show as they talked. Jackson felt disrespected when Sarah went to Emma for help instead of him, which made him defensive and a bit confrontational, making things worse.

On the other hand, Sarah felt overwhelmed and unsure about her tasks. She didn't want to look clueless, so she didn't ask Jackson for help and instead went to Emma, thinking it would be easier. When Jackson confronted her, she got defensive and a bit flippant, likely because she was frustrated and embarrassed. She felt Jackson's instructions weren't clear and didn't appreciate being criticized for not understanding them.

Jackson could have taken a different approach to keep things more positive. He could have taken a moment to calm down before talking to Sarah, which would have helped him stay neutral. If he had asked Sarah to share her perspective and challenges, it would have shown he was trying to understand her side. Instead of focusing on mistakes and communication gaps, Jackson could have given her constructive feedback and offered specific ways to improve.

To keep his cool better, Jackson could have paused, taken some deep breaths, or even taken a short walk to clear his head after overhearing Sarah's call. Approaching the conversation with empathy and acknowledging Sarah's challenges would have created a more positive interaction. Clear communication about his expectations and offering concrete steps for Sarah to improve would have been much more effective than showing his irritation.

Sarah, meanwhile, could have approached Jackson directly with her questions and concerns instead of avoiding him. Taking responsibility for her part in the miscommunication and showing a willingness to improve would have helped.

It's important to remember that both Jackson and Sarah are human, navigating their own challenges and imperfections. Despite all the inner work Jackson has been doing, he's still prone to moments of frustration. His efforts to practice mindfulness and personal growth don't make him immune to being triggered by stress and misunderstandings. In this instance, hearing Sarah's complaints hit a sore spot, and his human reaction was to feel defensive and upset.

Sarah is also human, dealing with the pressures of being a new employee and wanting to prove herself. Her hesitation to ask for help came from a place of wanting to seem capable, a very human and relatable feeling. When confronted, her defensive and flippant attitude was a knee-jerk reaction to her own feelings of inadequacy and frustration. Sarah's behavior reflects the natural human response to feeling pressured and misunderstood.

To make things right, Jackson and Sarah need to talk openly and honestly about their frustrations, challenges, and expectations. They should apologize for their mistakes and the way the conversation went and acknowledge their responsibilities regarding the event.

Forgiving each other involves developing empathy and compassion by putting themselves in each other's shoes and understanding the pressures and challenges each faces. They need to consciously decide to let go of any lingering resentment and focus on rebuilding a positive working relationship. Viewing the situation as a learning opportunity can help them move forward with a positive mindset.

Forgiving themselves requires self-reflection and recognizing that everyone makes mistakes. By practicing self-compassion and acknowledging their efforts and intentions, they can forgive themselves for not handling the situation perfectly. Committing to better communication and personal growth will enable them to move forward with renewed purpose and cooperation. This situation can be a stepping stone to building a stronger, more communicative working relationship.

Always forgive your enemies—
nothing annoys them so much.

—OSCAR WILDE

FUN AND EFFECTIVE GUIDE
TO RELEASE RESENTMENT AND RECLAIM JOY

1. Exercise: Perspective Taking

Exercise:

Imagine a person who hurt you and consider the situational pressures, their past, personality, provocations, and good intentions that led to their actions.

Ask Yourself Reflection Questions:

1. What situational pressures might have influenced their behavior?

2. What aspects of their past could have contributed to their actions?

3. How might their personality traits have played a role?

4. Did I do anything that might have been perceived as provocative?

5. What good intentions might they have had, even if their actions were hurtful?

Application Example:

Reflect on a conflict with a colleague and consider these prompts to understand their actions from a broader perspective.

Example for Jackson:

Jackson recalls the conflict with Sarah over her not coming to him for help. He considers the pressures Sarah might be under, such as getting used to being in a new position and personal issues, and realizes the behavior was not entirely personal but influenced by external stressors.

Example for Sarah:

Sarah thinks about the time when Jackson snapped at her. She considers Jackson's recent workload and personal challenges, understanding that his reaction was more about his own struggles than about her.

2. Exercise: Writing a Forgiveness Letter

Exercise:

Write a letter to the person who hurt you, expressing your feelings and the impact of their actions. Then, burn the letter as a symbolic act of letting go.

Ask Yourself Reflection Questions:

1. How did writing the letter make me feel?

2. What emotions surfaced as I described the impact of their actions?

3. How do I feel after burning the letter?

Application Example:

Write a letter to someone who caused you pain, noticing what specific feelings come up for you. Next, burn the letter to symbolize releasing those feelings and moving forward.

Example for Jackson:

Jackson writes a letter to Sarah, expressing his frustration and hurt from her words and reluctance to come to him for help. Burning the letter helps him feel a sense of release and clarity.

Example for Sarah:

Sarah writes a letter to Jackson detailing her fear of feeling inadequate in a new job. Burning the letter helps her let go of her anger, feel more at peace, and prepare for a fresh start.

3. Forgiveness and Other Meditation Practices

bit.ly/NMPmeditation

A FINAL THOUGHT TO PONDER
ABOUT THE PATHWAY TO INNER PEACE

Forgiveness is a word that often comes up when you think of someone else doing the forgiving. It can be very challenging, especially when life throws some of its harshest tests our way. The capacity to forgive is within all of us, but there will inevitably be moments when this is immensely difficult.

Consider, for example, the unimaginable pain of losing a loved one. The grief is overwhelming, and the anger toward the circumstances can make forgiveness seem impossible. Yet, forgiveness is the only way to experience true happiness again.

Imagine the deep betrayal of a spouse having an affair. The trust that once formed the foundation of the relationship is shattered, and the pain cuts deep. The pathway to forgiveness can be very difficult and twisted. Forgiveness doesn't have to mean forgetting or reconciling but letting go of the bitterness.

Even in more everyday scenarios, forgiveness has its place. Think about the frustration and anger that flare up when someone cuts you off in traffic. It might seem minor, but these small moments of anger accumulate and affect our overall well-being. Learning to forgive in these instances—recognizing that the other driver might be late picking up their mother from the doctor or a dad who's taking his kids' forgotten lunch to school—helps maintain our own serenity.

Forgiveness is also tested in situations where personal reputation is at stake. Imagine someone spreading vicious lies about you at work, leading to a tarnished reputation or even the loss of a job. The natural reaction is to seek revenge or harbor resentment. But forgiving the person who wronged you, as difficult as it might be, can liberate you from negativity. Instead of letting it destroy you, choose to forgive and move on; in doing so, maybe you'll even find your dream job.

What about the many instances of hateful racial comments or discriminatory behavior? These situations are particularly painful because they attack a core part of our identity. Forgiving someone who makes a racially motivated comment doesn't mean accepting or condoning their behavior. It means choosing not to carry the burden of their ignorance and hate. It's about taking the higher road and not allowing resentment to take root in your heart.

There are also moments when the offense is deeply personal, such as if a driver were to run over your dog. The grief of losing a pet can be as profound as losing a human loved one. You could choose to hold on to the anger, but instead, you forgive, understanding that harboring hate wouldn't bring your dog back but only prolong your pain.

Then there's the gut-wrenching story of the Amish community forgiving Charles Carl Roberts IV after the West Nickel Mines School shooting. This is a profound example of forgiveness on an immense scale. On October 2, 2006, Roberts entered a one-room Amish schoolhouse in Nickel Mines, Pennsylvania, armed with multiple weapons and shot ten girls, killing five, before taking his own life.

In the aftermath of the tragedy, the Amish community did something that seemed impossible—they forgave. They not only forgave the shooter but also reached out to his family with compassion. The Amish community attended Roberts' funeral, comforted his widow, and established a charitable fund for his children. It was an incredible act of grace and humanity that left me questioning my own capacity for forgiveness.

Forgiveness is not about the other person. It's about us—our hearts and minds, our peace and well-being. Whether it's a slight or a life-altering betrayal, learning to forgive is crucial. It's a journey that requires patience, empathy, and a willingness to let go of our pain.

So, what are you holding onto? Whatever it is, ask yourself what holding onto this anger and resentment is doing to you. Is it helping you, or is it holding you back?

Those who can let go are higher-level people. These forward-thinkers know deep down that holding onto grudges affects their peace and humanity.

By choosing to forgive, you not only free yourself from the burden of anger but also set an example for others to follow. Doing so doesn't mean forgetting or condoning the actions that hurt you. It means releasing those actions' hold on you and moving forward with a lighter heart. It means choosing peace over conflict and love over hate. It's about being the bigger, higher-level person who rises above the pettiness and pain.

In the end, the choice to forgive is a powerful one. It's a decision that transforms your life. So, take a moment to reflect on what you're holding onto, consider letting it go, and watch the doors open to new possibilities of happiness.

**The weak can never forgive.
Forgiveness is the attribute of the strong.**

—MAHATMA GANDHI

RESOURCES

HOW FORGIVENESS WORKS:
UNPACKING THE SCIENCE BEHIND LETTING GO

Let's explore how forgiveness can make a big difference in our lives, workplaces, and communities.

- **For Individuals:** Forgiving isn't just about saying, "It's okay." It's about choosing to let go of the anger that stresses you out or even makes you sick. When people hold on to negative feelings, it's like their body is gearing up for a battle—heart rate and blood pressure spike. But when they forgive, these stress responses often decrease, making them feel more relaxed and healthier. When we make forgiveness a practice, as we get older, we will forgive more often, which will lead to enjoying life more and feeling at ease. Research from Greater Good shows that engaging in forgiveness significantly reduces physiological stress responses.

- **In Relationships:** When our friends, family, or partners mess up, if we don't forgive them, inner turmoil will keep building up. Learning to forgive helps to keep our stress levels down and make our relationships stronger and more connected. It's important to understand that everyone makes mistakes, and holding grudges hurts us, too. Studies from the Greater Good have found that forgiveness in relationships reduces levels of cortisol, the stress hormone, leading to better health and happier interactions.

- **For Society:** When communities improve their forgiveness, everyone feels lighter and gets along better. Forgiveness programs demonstrate that people learn to let go of anger, leading to lower depression and anxiety and healthier communities. The British Psychological Society highlights that forgiveness helps manage stress more effectively, improving overall community mental health.

- **At Work:** Workplaces that cultivate forgiveness are generally more pleasant. If leaders and colleagues don't overreact to mistakes, it will create a relaxed and happy work environment. Employees are less afraid of making mistakes, which leads to better performance and longer tenure. Integrating forgiveness into corporate social responsibility boosts employee morale and attracts customers who value ethical practices, as discussed by IMD and Poppulo.

Forgiveness isn't just about moving past wrongs; it's about building stronger, healthier, and more productive environments. Whether in our personal lives, school, or in our jobs, forgiving significantly improves our interactions and well-being. It's like repairing a broken link so everyone continues moving forward interdependently.

EXAMPLES OF UNCHAINED LEADERS

- **Archbishop Desmond Tutu** is a beautiful example of forgiveness and reconciliation. His higher-level leadership during South Africa's turbulent journey toward equality displayed the healing power of forgiveness. As the head of the Truth and Reconciliation Commission, Tutu championed the idea that forgiveness is not a sign of weakness but a bold act of strength that bridges the deepest divides. His approach demonstrated that a higher form of leadership is not about asserting power but about unifying through understanding and grace.

- On the business side of things, **Bob Chapman's** approach at Barry-Wehmiller sums up "Truly Human Leadership." He believes in creating a workspace where every person feels valued, not just for their output but for their inherent worth. Chapman shows that leadership and compassion are inseparable by embracing a culture where mistakes are seen as chances to grow and where forgiveness is a pathway to innovation and loyalty. His methods highlight that forgiveness builds a thriving community within the workplace, proving that *"Allied We Can...Forgive Each Other."* It reported that his organization had $3.2 billion in 2022 revenue, with over 12,300 workers companywide.

Both leaders, in their unique arenas, serve up spiritually centered leadership that recognizes the healing power of forgiveness. Their lives and actions are shining examples of how leading with forgiveness is about moving past transgressions and elevating everyone to contribute their best with a spirit unhampered by resentment.

AUTHORS AND EXPERTS ON FORGIVENESS

- **Richard Rohr,** a renowned Franciscan priest and founder of the Center for Action and Contemplation, guides readers through the process of releasing egoic attachments and embracing forgiveness. Drawing on the wisdom of Saint Francis, Rohr offers a path to deeper freedom and divine connection. The audiobook *The Art of Letting Go* is a profound journey into the heart of true spiritual liberation.

- **Don Miguel Ruiz,** a renowned spiritual teacher and the author of *The Four Agreements,* shares Toltec wisdom through four practices: Be impeccable with your word, don't take anything personally, don't make assumptions, and always do your best.

This guide helps readers break self-limiting beliefs for a happier, more fulfilling life.

- **Donald B. Kraybill, Steven M. Nolt, and David L. Weaver-Zercher.** *Amish Grace* recounts the Amish community's profound act of forgiveness following the 2006 Nickel Mines schoolhouse shooting, offering deep insights into their faith and resilience. This moving story challenges readers to understand and embody true forgiveness.

- **Dr. Robert Enright** is a pioneer in the scientific study of forgiveness. He has authored numerous books, including *Forgiveness is a Choice,* which provides a step-by-step process for learning how to forgive.

- **Dr. Fred Luskin** is the director of the Stanford Forgiveness Projects and the author of *Forgive for Good*, a book based on his research into the benefits of forgiveness.

- **Desmond Tutu** co-wrote *The Book of Forgiving* with his daughter, Mpho Tutu. It offers practical advice and profound insights into the reasons for forgiveness and its impact on one's life.

Chapter 6:
Practice Six, Genuine

THE SPIRITUALLY CENTERED HIGHER-LEVEL GROUNDED AND STEADY LEADER

ELEMENT ONE: GROUNDED AND STEADY ✑

BUILD A SOLID FOUNDATION OF TRUST AND INTEGRITY, PROVIDING STABILITY AND CONSISTENCY IN LEADERSHIP

It was an early August Saturday morning, and I was sitting on the wrap-around porch enjoying the view while watching my wildlife friends go about their business. Over by the horse pasture sat a gaggle of Canadian geese, who, earlier in the week, had to share their grubs with Sandhill cranes. There's an array of wildlife that visits every day, it seems like a new species shows up. Maybe I should start charging admission to see our wildlife.

I was having coffee, thinking about my plans for the day. Grocery shopping was a priority, and I was adding last-minute items to the list. I wanted to get my least favorite chore done quickly so I could hop on my gravel bike for a spin before the heat of the day set in. I also thought about going kayaking that evening to splash around on the lake and cool off. Feeling antsy, I headed out to get my SUV washed before going to my first stop.

By the time I got to the checkout at the grocery store, I was ready to escape the crowds and get on my bike. Just after getting my bill's total, I looked up and saw her. This Gerber redhead baby girl was sitting in her mom's grocery cart, cooing with a radiant smile on her face. She was living in the moment, with no concerns about the grocery bill and no rush to go somewhere else to have fun. She was having fun doing what babies do.

On the other hand, her mom was a hot mess, trying to round up her toddler siblings. I made eye contact with the baby and immediately became fully present. I didn't wish to be somewhere else or hope the cashier would hurry up so I could get on my bike. I was witnessing an example of true authenticity. The baby wasn't trying to look cute; she was just cute. She wasn't trying to act like or be like anyone else. She was herself. She wasn't trying to fit in with any group; she was showing up as she was, take it or leave it. She wasn't trying to hide any behavior that could be judged; she was behaving unapologetically.

The wildlife in the yard live out their true selves, the cranes do their crane thing, tearing up the yard looking for a meal of grubs. They don't care that it annoys me that they're ripping up my manicured lawn. The baby fawn chasing after its mother is being herself without regard to how she looks when she runs, even though it's awkward. The eleven turkeys in the flock aren't a bit concerned about how the members of their group look or behave. What do the baby girl and the wildlife all have in common? They are being who they are. No apologies, no shame, no guilt. They're all being true to themselves.

THE DIFFERENT MASKS WE WEAR

In his book *The Masks We Wear,* Keith Blakemore-Noble talks about the different personas we adopt in various social, professional, and personal situations. He explains that we wear these masks due to societal pressures, fear of judgment, and the desire to fit in. These masks become obstacles to genuine self-expression and meaningful connections, leading to feelings of inauthenticity and dissatisfaction. Keith highlights the importance of self-awareness and being true to ourselves.

As I stood in the checkout line, making eye contact with that baby girl, I realized that she wasn't burdened by any masks. She was simply being herself, boldly authentic, without filters or apologies. It reminded me that we, too, can strive to drop the masks we wear and embrace our true selves. Just like the wildlife in our yard, living freely and authentically, we find joy and fulfillment in being who we truly are.

When Do We Start Wearing These Masks?

Babies as young as 15 months cry, knowing their parents will come to pick them up. In a 2018 study, 188 multidisciplinary teachers in Russian preschools, "The Age and Psychological Conditions of the Manipulative Behavior of Preschool Children," observed 160 common childhood maneuvers among kids ages three to seven.

Children's ability to follow rules and adapt their behavior in different settings develops through a mix of thinking, emotions, and social interactions. From infancy, they start responding to simple caregiver requests and looking for social cues. As toddlers, they begin to understand basic rules and act differently depending on where they are. During preschool years, they internalize rules and show self-control, influenced by how their parents raise them. They also learn to behave differently in various settings, like being quieter in a classroom and more free-spirited on a playground.

By school age, children grasp more complex rules and social norms, learning to differentiate between moral rules (like not biting their friends), social rules (like saying "please" and "thank you"), and personal choices (like picking out their own clothes). They adjust their behavior based on the social context, such as being polite at a family gathering and more relaxed with friends. Parenting style, social environment, and their own cognitive and emotional development play a big role in this process.

In college, we adapt our behavior to fit into different social settings. A student might act studious in the classroom but become the life of the party at a dorm gathering. Similarly, when we date, we put on different masks based on our interest level, being extra polite and attentive on a first date but more relaxed on a later, more casual one.

We also wear different masks in various settings like church, work, and family gatherings. At church, people might act more reverent and reserved, aligning with the expectations of the congregation. Someone might adopt a formal tone and dress in business attire to maintain a professional image at work. Around parents, we might act more responsible and mature to appear dependable, even if we enjoy carefree activities with friends.

On social media, our interactions can differ significantly from in-person behavior. Someone might curate their profile online to highlight only the best aspects of their life and engage in debates or express opinions more freely behind the screen. This online mask can be very different from how they behave face-to-face, where immediate reactions and real-time interactions shape the conversation.

At What Point Do We Lose Who We Are?

With all these different masks we wear, it's easy to forget our true selves. Who we genuinely are becomes buried under layers of changing behavior. When we constantly shift our actions and attitudes to fit different roles and expectations, we risk losing touch with what makes us unique. The challenge is balancing the need to adapt while staying true to ourselves, making sure our core identity stays intact and visible.

Authentic and Genuine Leaders

Even though we wear masks, there are great examples of people who stay genuine, showing that authenticity and integrity exist in our different roles. Steve Jobs, the co-founder of Apple, was known for his honest and passionate approach to innovation. He wasn't perfect and didn't try to be, but his true commitment to his vision inspired people to push boundaries and strive for excellence. Jobs showed that being genuine isn't about being flawless; it's about staying true to your principles and inspiring others.

Nelson Mandela is another example of someone with strong integrity and a real concern for justice and equality. Even with huge personal sacrifices, Mandela's dedication to his principles helped end apartheid and heal a divided nation. His story teaches us that real integrity in leadership leads to deep, lasting change.

Similarly, Estée Lauder, an American entrepreneur and one of the largest players in the beauty business was known for her honest communication style. She wasn't afraid to share her personal journey and struggles, which made her relatable and admired by her employees. This kind of open and honest communication creates a refreshing and trustworthy environment.

Unmasking True Values After Life Shocks

Often, a significant event makes us question our true higher intent and reassess our values and beliefs. This might be a personal loss, a major life change, or an unexpected challenge that forces us to pause and reflect. For example, discovering that a spouse or partner had an affair can be a profound emotional shock that opens us up to reflect on our relationship and our own identity. The loss of a loved one leads us to re-evaluate our priorities and what we truly value in life. Being kicked out of a group we belong to makes us question our sense of belonging and who we are without that social validation. Being fired from a job challenges our sense of purpose and forces us to consider what truly fulfills us. Similarly, the loss of wealth prompts us to reassess what brings real happiness and meaning to our lives. Such moments strip away the masks we've been wearing and reveal what really matters to us.

Will the Real Eric Miller Please Stand Up?

My name is Eric, and I'm a grateful recovering alcoholic and drug addict. In 2015, significant events propelled me into redefining who I was and my core values. It took the demise of a personal relationship and the loss of someone I deeply loved dying of cancer. Addiction, no matter what form it takes, creeps up on you. It certainly did with me. At a very young age, I used alcohol to help me feel safe. Later, I added drugs to change any unwanted emotional states, like self-doubt and high levels of anxiety.

I wrote above that I'm grateful, which is true because it had to become painful enough for me to change how I dealt with emotions and events. When I became completely sober, I had to figure out new healthy ways to cope with stress and everything else that life presents. I quickly realized that the thinking that got me in the mess that I created would not get me out of it. I had to become self-aware and vulnerable with God and seek different types of therapies and programs. I also accepted help from a mentor and coach. I was then able to take responsibility and become accountable for the harm that I had caused. And what was most liberating for me was making things right wherever I could.

Finding My True North and Genuine Living

Making the decision to redefine who I was and what being authentic meant to me was a significant moment. It was turning a new page in my life, where I committed to being true to myself and my values. Let me share how I began and what I learned along the way.

Self-Reflection

I started by setting aside quiet moments each day to reflect on my thoughts and feelings. This helped me become more aware of my emotions and the things that truly mattered to me. I examined every area of my life and questioned my beliefs. Byron Katie, the author of *Loving What Is,* developed a self-inquiry method known as *"The Work,"* which centers on four key questions designed to help individuals challenge and transform their negative thoughts.

Ask four simple questions about any belief that causes you pain:

1. Is it true?

2. Can you absolutely know that it's true?

3. How do you react, what happens when you believe that thought?

4. Who would you be without the thought?

These questions helped me examine my thoughts critically, understand the impact of my beliefs, and envision a life without these limiting thoughts. After going through these questions, I went through a process called "turnaround," where I reversed my thoughts to understand how my perceptions created my reality. On many occasions, I found the truth in the opposite of my original thought.

Recalibrating My Values

Doing the work using Byron Katie's approach, getting coaching help, and reading lots of books helped me reevaluate what was most important to me. My values have changed dramatically since getting sober. I didn't really know who I was or what I believed before that.

bit.ly/NMPvalues

The life-changing event of putting down the pipe and putting a "plug in the jug" made me question and later forget much of what I thought was true. I needed to find out what mattered to me the most. I wanted to be as genuine as that baby in the grocery store. That's why I created the **Values in Motion: Assessing What's Most Important**—to help others do the same work of uncovering their true values.

Next, I focused on identifying my values. These are the beliefs that guide my actions and decisions. By reflecting on different aspects of my life, I was able to determine what truly matters to me. I used values elicitation exercises, which helped me discover my core values. Once I identified these values, I took practical steps to align every part of my life with them—relationships, career, finances, and spirituality. The Values in Motion assessment now provides a clear path for others to take these same life-changing steps.

Aligning Life with Values

True fulfillment comes from living in alignment with your most meaningful values and remaining true to yourself. I assessed my relationships to ensure they aligned with my values of honesty and compassion. In my career, I focused on opportunities that allowed me to stay true to my value of helping others. Financially, I aimed for decisions that reflected my value of security and responsibility.

Spiritually, I ensured my practices were in line with my belief in personal growth and inner peace.

To implement these changes, I created an action plan with specific steps and timelines. I made lifestyle changes to reflect my values in daily routines, like dedicating time to personal development and ensuring my actions at work were aligned with my values. I regularly reviewed my values and checked if my life was still in alignment with them. As my values evolved, I adjusted my goals and actions accordingly.

bit.ly/valuesactionplan

Embracing Challenges and Honesty

Facing my fears was another crucial step. Being authentic often means stepping out of your comfort zone. Whether it was speaking up in a group or admitting when I was wrong, I learned to embrace these challenges. Each time I did, I felt a bit more confident and truer to myself.

Honesty became a cornerstone of my journey. I made a conscious effort to be truthful, not only with others but also with myself. If I made a mistake, I owned up to it and tried to learn from it. This honesty built trust in my relationships and made me feel more grounded.

Self-Love and Respect for Others

Loving myself, flaws and all, was also important. I realized that everyone has imperfections, and that's okay. I built a healthier self-esteem by treating myself with the same kindness and understanding I offered others. This self-acceptance allows me to be more genuine and less worried about what others think.

Lastly, respecting others played a vital role in my path to authenticity. I learned to accept people for who they are, even if their beliefs or behaviors differed from mine. This respect enriched my interactions and broadened my perspective.

Ongoing Journey

Becoming more genuine and authentic and living with integrity is an ongoing process. It's about continuously learning, reflecting, and aligning your actions with your true self and values. Am I always true to myself and my values in all of my actions? No, I'm not. The difference is that I'm more aware when I misstep and take action to get back on track. This is a journey that makes me feel more confident and truer to myself, and I continue to discover new things about who I am every day.

Integrity is doing the right thing,
even when no one is watching.

—C.S. LEWIS

MORE INSPIRING EXAMPLES

Many have undertaken the journey of living an authentic life with integrity and self-respect. Albert Einstein and Eleanor Roosevelt are two more inspiring figures who exemplified these qualities. Both faced big challenges and stayed true to their values, making a huge impact on the world. Einstein, with his amazing scientific discoveries and commitment to peace, and Roosevelt, fighting for social justice and human rights, showed us what it means to live genuinely and with integrity. Being true to ourselves and our principles leads to meaningful and lasting change.

Eleanor Roosevelt: Champion of Social Justice and Integrity

Eleanor Roosevelt, one of the most influential women of the 20th century, was celebrated not only for her role as the First Lady of the United States but also for her unwavering commitment to social justice, human rights, and integrity. Born in 1884 into a prominent family, Eleanor's early life was marked by personal tragedy, including the loss of both parents by the age of ten. These hardships shaped her empathetic nature and a strong sense of duty to others.

As First Lady from 1933 to 1945, Eleanor redefined the role into a platform for advocacy and activism. She was genuine in her commitment to addressing social issues, including poverty, racial discrimination, and women's rights. Unlike previous First Ladies, she actively engaged with the public, traveling extensively to understand the struggles of ordinary Americans during the Great Depression. Her syndicated column, "My Day," was published from 1935 to 1962 and reached millions. It provided a candid look into her thoughts and activities, reflecting her authenticity and transparency.

Eleanor's integrity was evident in her steadfast support for civil rights. At a time when segregation was rampant, she defied societal norms by advocating for African Americans. In 1939, she publicly resigned from the Daughters of the American Revolution after they refused to allow African American singer Marian Anderson to perform at Constitution Hall. She then arranged for Anderson to sing at the Lincoln Memorial, making a powerful statement against racial injustice.

After Franklin Roosevelt's death, Eleanor continued her public service on the global stage. As a delegate to the United Nations, she chaired the committee that drafted the Universal Declaration of Human Rights, adopted in 1948. Her work was driven by a deep belief in equality and justice, reflecting her genuine commitment to human dignity.

Eleanor's personal life also mirrored her authenticity. Despite facing criticism and resistance, she remained true to her values, encouraging an environment of openness and progressive thinking. She famously said, *"Do what you feel in your heart to be right—for you'll be criticized anyway."*

Eleanor's legacy is defined by her relentless advocacy for social justice and human rights, her authenticity in addressing the issues of her time, and her integrity in standing by her principles. Her life serves as an enduring example of how she used her platform to effect meaningful change, staying true to herself.

Einstein's True North: A Journey of Genius and Integrity

Albert Einstein was a groundbreaking scientist who revolutionized 20th-century physics. Born in 1879 in Ulm, Germany, he is famous for his theory of relativity, which changed how we understand space, time, and energy. But Einstein was more than just a brilliant scientist; he was also a person of great character.

Einstein was relentless in his pursuit of truth. He wasn't interested in becoming famous or winning awards. Instead, he was curious about how the universe works. This curiosity led him to question things that most people accepted as true. His famous equation, E=mc2, showed his ability to think differently and explore new ideas. He often said that imagination and curiosity were more important than just memorizing facts, inspiring many people to think creatively.

Einstein's honesty and principles were evident in everything he did. He stood up for peace and human rights, using his fame to speak against injustice. When fascism rose in Germany, he moved to the United States in 1933 to stay true to his beliefs. In the U.S., he supported civil rights and worked with the NAACP. He even wrote letters to important African American leaders like W.E.B. Du Bois. After seeing the destruction caused by atomic bombs in World War II, Einstein pushed for nuclear disarmament, showing his commitment to doing what was right.

Einstein was also quite genuine in his personal life. Despite being famous, he stayed humble and friendly. He often wrote back to young students who reached out to him. His playful sense of humor and straightforward way of talking made people like him. One of his famous quotes is, *"The important thing is not to stop questioning. Curiosity has its own reason for existing."* This shows his love for learning and his belief in always asking questions.

In the end, Albert Einstein's legacy isn't just about his scientific discoveries. It's also about his honesty, his courage, and his commitment to staying true to himself. His life reminds us that authenticity and integrity are just as important as being smart. Einstein's story inspires us to live with curiosity, stand up for what we believe in, and always stay true to who we are.

Try not to become a man of success,
but rather try to become a man of value.

—ALBERT EINSTEIN

TRUE TO YOU:
WRAPPING UP THE QUEST FOR
GENUINE HIGHER-LEVEL LEADERSHIP

Throughout our lives, we go through experiences that change how we see the world and what we care about. Our values aren't fixed; they grow and change as we do. Someone once told me, *"My parents taught me my values as a kid, so why would I change?"* But as we grow up, it's natural for our priorities and values to evolve.

We can't always be our true selves in every situation; sometimes, we have to wear masks that fit the moment. What's important is to stay true to who we are, even when we have to adapt. Think about Steve Jobs. When he was kicked out of Apple, he didn't give up. Instead, he came back even stronger and more creative. Nelson Mandela spent 27 years in prison, but that only made him more determined to end apartheid. Eleanor Roosevelt lost her parents when she was very young, which made her passionate about fighting for social justice. Albert Einstein faced many rejections early in his career, but he kept pushing the boundaries of science. These remarkable people were shaped by their challenges, which fueled their incredible achievements.

When we face rejection or challenges, we question who we are and whether we're living in line with our true selves or just trying to fit in. These moments can be turning points, helping us rediscover our values and commit to living authentically. They remind us that our true identity comes from our inner beliefs and values, not from what others think of us.

Being part of a group, whether it's a political party or a social circle, gives us a sense of belonging. It feels good to support our group's ideas and leaders. But sometimes, this loyalty leads to division and conflict. People often support their party blindly in politics, creating an "us vs. them" mentality. This divisiveness and refusal to listen to other viewpoints makes it hard to find common ground. In social groups, we might stick to our own circle and miss out on the value of other perspectives.

To deal with these challenges, staying open-minded and including different perspectives while being true to ourselves is important. Talking to people from different groups and listening to their opinions helps us bridge divides. Being genuine ensures that our relationships are based on honesty and respect, which deepens connections.

Higher-level leadership means being genuine and leading with integrity. Authentic leaders inspire trust and respect because they stay true to their values and are open about their actions. They face challenges head-on, admit their mistakes, and learn from them.

Living genuinely and authentically is ongoing. It requires continuous self-reflection, a commitment to personal growth, and a willingness to accept change. When we use our challenges to grow and inspire others, we become the action that drives change. By staying true to ourselves and our values, we can start a chain reaction that has no end.

RESOURCES

AUTHORS AND EXPERTS ON INTEGRITY AND AUTHENTICITY

Living with more integrity and authenticity is a continual process of self-discovery and self-expression. It involves having the courage to live by your values and beliefs, being true to yourself, and building deeper connections with others. Here are some resources you can use to cultivate spiritually centered, higher-level leadership.

BOOKS ON INTEGRITY AND AUTHENTICITY

The Way of Integrity: Finding the Path to Your True Self by **Martha Beck** – This book explores the concept of living in alignment with one's true self. Beck integrates elements from Dante's "Divine Comedy" to guide readers through the process of aligning their actions with their inner truth, which she argues is crucial for personal happiness and integrity (PositivePsychology.com).

The Integrity Advantage by **Kelley Kosow** – Kosow's book offers a fresh look at how living with integrity involves more than just honesty—it's about living congruently with your values and beliefs. The book provides practical steps for transforming your life through a commitment to integrity (Paul Finch Unofficial Author Website).

Integrity: The Courage to Meet the Demands of Reality by **Dr. Henry Cloud** – In this book, Dr. Cloud discusses how integrity involves the courage to face reality and the six qualities of character that define it. He emphasizes that integrity is not just about being honest but also about meeting the demands of reality (Paul Finch Unofficial Author Website).

***Authentic Leadership* (Harvard Business Review Emotional Intelligence Series)** – This collection of articles from the Harvard Business Review discusses the importance of emotional intelligence in leadership and how authenticity in leadership involves balancing vulnerability with authority (PositivePsychology.com).

***The Integrity of the Judge* by David Pimentel** – Pimentel offers a thought-provoking exploration of integrity within the judiciary, discussing the complex web of ethics, honesty, and moral practices that underpin the functioning of a just society (Paul Finch Unofficial Author Website).

Chapter 7:
Practice Seven, Accountable

THE SPIRITUALLY CENTERED HIGHER-LEVEL PASSIONATE AND INSPIRING LEADER

ELEMENT FOUR: PASSIONATE AND INSPIRING ⚱

IGNITE PASSION AND DRIVE WITHIN OTHERS, INSPIRING CREATIVITY AND MOTIVATION

Leading effectively at a higher level requires being genuine and maintaining integrity. Authentic people build trust and respect by being true to their values and transparent about their actions. They confront difficulties head-on, acknowledge their errors, do their best to fix what went wrong, and grow from them. I've said it before, but it bears repeating: living authentically is an ongoing journey that requires constant self-reflection, a dedication to personal development, and a readiness to adapt to change. Staying true to our core values can set off a ripple effect and influence a whole nation.

Angela Merkel, the former chancellor of Germany, exemplifies high-level leadership. Her tenure was marked by careful planning and a commitment to keeping Europe united. This approach earned her widespread trust and led to effective governance. Merkel demonstrated resilience and innovation, guiding Germany and Europe through numerous challenges. Even during difficult times, her steadfast dedication shows us that responsibility leads to tremendous success.

As the first woman to become chancellor of Germany, she worked tirelessly to ensure the well-being of her country and the European Union. Merkel's commitment to her people and principles allowed her to lead with integrity and dedication. Her story shows that true leadership involves being faithful to one's values and the greater good, even under the most challenging circumstances.

Throughout her time in office, Merkel faced many personal and public challenges but never avoided her duty to advocate for social justice and human rights. She used her platform to drive significant change. Despite criticism, her relentless pursuit of justice reinforced that being responsible means standing by your principles and using your influence to make a positive impact.

In my own journey, I've learned that being responsible and accountable means continuously evaluating my actions and their impact. It involves being honest about my mistakes, learning from them, and making amends when necessary. This ongoing process of self-reflection helps me align my actions with my values.

Accountability breeds response-ability.

—STEPHEN R. COVEY

OWNING IT AFTER DOING IT

Differentiating between responsibility and accountability can get a little cloudy; even though they're similar, their meanings are different.

Responsibility is about the tasks or duties you're supposed to do. It's about your role or job and what you need to do to get it done. For example, a teacher is responsible for making lesson plans, teaching students, and grading papers. These are the tasks that come with their job.

Accountability is taking ownership of what happens because of your responsibilities. It's about being answerable for the results of your actions, whether they're good or bad. Accountability means admitting when things go wrong and working to fix them. For example, if students in the teacher's class do poorly on a test, the teacher is accountable for finding out why and making changes to help them do better next time.

Let me share a personal story to further explain. After the misunderstanding with my helpmate that I mentioned in Chapter 5, I realized that I needed to apologize and make things right with him. I had delegated certain tasks to my helper, tasks for which I was ultimately responsible. When things went wrong, I knew it was my duty to address the situation and ensure it was corrected. Apologizing was difficult, but it was a necessary step in mending the relationship. As I sought to understand his perspective, our conversation deepened, and we uncovered cultural differences that had contributed to the issue. Specifically, the language barrier with the IT person had played a significant role. We realized that what seemed like a simple miscommunication was, in fact, rooted in differing cultural norms around communication, expectations, and even problem-solving approaches. By recognizing these differences and discussing them openly, we were able to bridge the gap, fostering a better working relationship and deeper mutual understanding.

This personal example shows how responsibility and accountability work together. I took responsibility for doing my job and was accountable for making things right when things didn't go well. My willingness to apologize and make amends led to more trust and respect among the team and Walter.

The price of greatness is responsibility.

—WINSTON CHURCHILL

NOT OWNING IT, AFTER DOING IT

So, what do we do when someone makes a mistake and doesn't hold themselves accountable when things don't go as planned? I think most of us have been on both sides of this. There have been times when we didn't take ownership of something we were in charge of, and other times when someone else didn't own up to their part when things went wrong. What do we do?

In either case, we do some self-reflection and look for our part in the situation. Then, we take measures to make it right. For example, if a project didn't meet its deadline because we failed to communicate effectively, we should acknowledge our mistake, apologize to the team, and come up with a plan to improve communication in the future.

But what do we do when someone else doesn't hold themselves accountable? First, we should address the issue calmly and directly with the person involved, expressing how their actions impacted the project and the team. We offer support to help them improve, such as providing additional training or resources. By addressing the issue constructively, we encourage accountability.

In Chapter 5, a conflict arose between Sarah and Jackson. Feeling self-conscious and not asking for help before making a mistake on a project, Sarah complained to her mother about Jackson's unclear instructions. Instead of seeking clarification directly from him, she went to Emma for help after the fact. Jackson overheard the conversation, which made him feel disrespected and frustrated.

When Jackson confronted Sarah, his irritation surfaced, leading to a defensive and flippant response from her. The emotional reaction from both sides escalated the tension between them. Reflecting on their behavior, Jackson and Sarah realized they needed to be accountable for their actions. They both were open to having another conversation. Each of them understood that addressing their mistakes openly and honestly was essential for moving forward. With this in mind, Jackson decided to approach Sarah again, with a genuine desire to reconcile. Sarah, too, was prepared to be accountable for her part in the conversation. Here's how it went.

The day after they had clashed, Jackson walked over to Sarah's desk, taking a deep breath to steady himself. *"Hey Sarah, can we talk for a minute?"* he asked, trying to keep his voice calm and inviting.

Sarah looked up from her desk, a bit surprised, but nodded. *"Sure, Jackson."*

He sat down next to her desk. *"I wanted to apologize for how I handled things yesterday. I lost my cool, and that wasn't fair to you. I've been doing a lot of inner work, but I'm still human, and sometimes, my emotions get the best of me."*

Sarah looked down, feeling a mix of relief and guilt. *"Thanks, Jackson. I appreciate that. I guess I didn't handle it well either. I was frustrated and overwhelmed and didn't want to look incompetent. I should have been more accountable and come to you with my questions instead of complaining about it."*

Jackson nodded, appreciating her honesty. *"It's easy to let emotions take over, especially when we're under pressure. I felt disrespected when you went to Emma instead of me, but I realize now that my instructions might not have been as clear as they should have been. I'm committed to improving and being more approachable."*

Sarah sighed, feeling a weight lift off her shoulders. *"I was trying to prove myself and didn't want to seem like I couldn't handle it. I should have communicated better and asked for help. I'm sorry for being defensive and flippant."*

Jackson smiled gently. *"We're both learning how to work together, Sarah. It's important to remember that we're imperfect people, and that's okay. What's crucial is that we learn from these moments. Let's make a pact to be more open with each other and communicate our needs and expectations clearly."*

Sarah nodded, a small smile forming on her lips. *"Deal. I'll make sure to come to you with any questions or concerns from now on. And I'll work on being more accountable for my actions."*

They both stood up, and Jackson extended his hand. Sarah shook it, feeling a renewed sense of cooperation and understanding. As Jackson left, they both felt lighter and more connected, ready to move forward with a positive mindset.

This honest conversation helped them reconcile and forgive each other. They recognized their humanity and imperfections and, by doing so, set the foundation for a better working relationship. They also committed to forgiving themselves for not handling the situation perfectly, knowing that their efforts and intentions were genuine.

He that is good for making excuses
is seldom good for anything else.

—BENJAMIN FRANKLIN

FROM FLAKE TO FANTASTIC: YOUR GUIDE TO ROCK-SOLID RESPONSIBILITY AND UNSHAKEABLE ACCOUNTABILITY

Introduction to the Guide on Responsibility and Accountability

Imagine a homeowner who enjoys decorating and renovating their house but sometimes neglects routine maintenance. When things go wrong, this person may blame external factors like weather or poor construction rather than acknowledging their lack of preparation. This scenario mirrors how people with less responsibility often struggle with impulsiveness and reliability.

In contrast, consider a homeowner who follows maintenance schedules and knows their house well. They understand the importance of regular upkeep and planning, though they may sometimes get caught off guard by unexpected issues. Most of the time, they manage to keep their home in good condition, ensuring everyone's safety while learning to adapt to the demands of homeownership.

Finally, think of a seasoned homeowner who meticulously plans every renovation and regularly checks their home's condition. They excel at decision-making, risk management, and keeping their family informed and prepared. These homeowners take complete responsibility for their home's upkeep and rarely, if ever, blame others for setbacks. By developing similar traits of responsibility and accountability, you will build trust and reliability in both personal and professional relationships. This guide provides practical steps and activities to help you enhance these traits, ensuring you're well-prepared to tackle life's challenges with integrity.

1. Understanding Responsibility and Accountability

Goal: *Grasp the fundamental concepts of personal responsibility and accountability and their significance.*

Activity:

- Research and write down the definitions of personal responsibility and accountability.

- List five benefits of being responsible and accountable personally and professionally.

Why This Matters:

Understanding these concepts is the foundation for understanding the importance of personal responsibility and accountability in various aspects of life. Knowing the benefits is motivational for adopting these traits.

Reflection:

Reflect on a recent situation where you did not act responsibly or failed to be accountable. Write down what you could have done differently to handle the situation better.

Example Application:

Recognize the importance of accountability in your daily life. For instance, if you missed a work deadline, identify why and think about how better planning could have prevented it.

Example Application for Sarah and Jackson:

- **Sarah:** Reflects on her mistakes and realizes she should have sought clarification from Jackson directly instead of complaining to her mother and seeking help from Emma. She acknowledges that asking for help earlier would have prevented the mistake.

- **Jackson:** Reflects on how his irritation in confronting Sarah escalated the situation. He realizes that approaching Sarah calmly and seeking a solution together would have been more effective.

2. Implementing Strategies for Accountability

Goal: *Apply practical methods to enhance personal accountability in daily activities.*

Activity:

- Identify three methods to improve accountability, such as putting notes on your mirror, nightstand, or screen saver, using a planner, setting reminders, seeking feedback from peers, or hiring a coach.

- Apply these methods in your daily routine. For example, use a digital calendar to set deadlines and reminders.

Why This Matters:

Implementing practical strategies helps create a structured approach to managing responsibilities effectively and a habit of accountability.

Reflection:

At the end of the week, review your progress. Did you meet your goals? What worked well, and what didn't?

Example Application:

Set daily reminders for important tasks and use a planner to keep track of your responsibilities. Seek feedback from a colleague or friend at the end of the week to assess your progress.

Example Application for Sarah and Jackson:

- **Sarah:** Uses a digital planner to schedule times for checking in with teammates about project tasks. She sets daily reminders to review her progress and ensure she understands all instructions before starting work.

- **Jackson:** Implements a weekly check-in with Sarah to provide clear instructions and address any questions she might have. He sets reminders to prepare for these meetings and reviews their progress together.

3. Creating a Personal Mission Statement

Goal: *Develop a personal mission statement that outlines your core values and commitment to accountability.*

Activity:

- Draft a personal mission statement that highlights how you plan to stay accountable and responsible in your actions. It doesn't need to be perfect or formal—just a few simple, honest sentences or a quick list of your values and goals will work. The key is to make sure it truly reflects your commitment to owning your choices and actions.

- Share your mission statement with a trusted friend or colleague for feedback and support.

Why This Matters:

A mission statement serves as a constant reminder of your values and goals. Sharing it with others increases your commitment to it.

Reflection:

Reflect on how your mission statement aligns with your daily actions and decisions. Adjust your actions if they do not align with your stated mission.

Example Application:

Write a mission statement such as, *"I commit to being reliable and accountable in all my actions to build trust and integrity."* Share it with a friend and ask for their input.

Example Application for Sarah and Jackson:

- **Sarah:** "My mission is to practice proactive communication and actively seek help when needed. I am committed to improving my accountability and ensuring transparency with my team."

- **Jackson:** "My mission is to maintain open, respectful communication, especially in challenging situations. I am dedicated to resolving conflicts constructively and fostering a positive working relationship with my team and superiors."

4. Long-Term Goal Planning

Goal: *Develop a more detailed plan to achieve a long-term goal by breaking it into smaller, manageable tasks.*

Activity:

Identify a long-term goal and break it down into smaller tasks with specific deadlines.

Create a timeline for completing each task and set reminders to review your progress regularly.

Why This Matters:

Breaking down a long-term goal into smaller tasks makes it more manageable and less overwhelming. Regular reviews help you stay on track.

Reflection:

Assess your monthly progress toward the long-term goal. Reflect on how increased accountability influenced your success and identify areas for improvement.

Example Application:

Set a long-term goal, such as completing a professional certification, and break it down into monthly study targets. Use a calendar to track deadlines and set regular review dates.

Example Application:

- **Sarah:** Sets a long-term goal of improving her project management skills to better handle complex projects at work. To make it achievable, she breaks it into smaller, monthly milestones, such as completing an online course on project management and then applying specific techniques—like setting clearer deadlines and using new project tracking tools—on her current projects. Each week, Sarah reviews her progress by checking how well her projects are running and gathering feedback from her team. If she notices areas that need improvement, she makes adjustments to her plan, such as focusing more on time management or team communication for the next month.

- **Jackson:** Wants to develop his leadership skills to create a more cohesive and motivated team. He enrolls in a leadership training program where he learns strategies like active listening, conflict resolution, and giving constructive feedback. Jackson sets quarterly goals to practice these skills with his team, starting with holding regular one-on-one feedback sessions with team members, including Sarah. He uses these sessions to ensure that everyone is on the same page, fostering open communication and addressing any concerns. After each quarter, Jackson reflects on the team's progress and considers new leadership techniques to further strengthen team dynamics.

IMMEDIATE IMPROVEMENT TIPS:

1. **Use a Planner:** Start each day by listing your tasks and prioritizing them.

2. **Set Reminders:** Use digital reminders to keep track of deadlines.

3. **Seek Feedback:** Regularly ask a trusted friend or colleague for feedback on your progress.

4. **Reflect Daily:** Spend 5-10 minutes each evening reflecting on what you accomplished and what could be improved.

5. **Stay Consistent:** Consistency is key. Make these activities a daily habit.

By implementing the four steps in this guide, you'll see improvements in your personal responsibility and accountability, leading to better outcomes in your personal and professional life.

HOW PASSION AND RESPONSIBILITY MAKES YOU UNSTOPPABLE

We often see examples of people who avoid taking responsibility for their actions. In politics, for instance, there are leaders who make promises they never intend to keep, shifting blame to others when things go wrong. In the corporate world, some executives prioritize profit over ethics, neglecting the impact of their decisions on employees, customers, and even the environment. Some athletes cheat because they are so focused on winning that they betray their values. In our personal lives, we encounter individuals who refuse to admit their mistakes, choosing instead to place the blame elsewhere.

But through all the muck, some people hold themselves accountable for their actions. They're grounded and steady in their values and do the hard things, even when no one is watching. They're also doing things for others that we may never hear about until a news story or social media post talks about an anonymous person who did this remarkable thing.

These higher-level individuals consistently do the right thing because it's who they are. They don't think of themselves as heroes; to them, there is no other way of behaving. Perhaps they weren't always like that, but an event shocked them to their core, and they decided to do something about it and change. They redefined their values, were true to themselves, and now cared deeply about certain things.

Throughout the different stages of my life, I've asked myself what I truly care about. What drives me to get up each day and strive for something better? Passion is a powerful thing. It pushes us to go after our dreams and tackle challenges that seem impossible. When you care about something, you pour your heart into it, dedicating time and energy to making it happen. But passion alone isn't enough, and a dream can be just that—a dream.

What are you passionate about? Is there something you really care about and want to change in the world? Maybe there's a goal you've been dreaming of achieving or a challenge you've faced that you want to help others overcome. Think about those moments when you felt a spark of inspiration, those times when you knew deep down that you could make a real difference. Maybe you want to improve your community, protect the environment, or fight for social justice. It's about realizing that your efforts matter and that you have the power to make a positive impact.

Think about a tough challenge you've overcome. Maybe it was a personal struggle, a difficult situation, or a setback that tested your limits. Overcoming such challenges teaches us important lessons and makes us stronger.

Let me share an example that has inspired me. Imagine a young man who loves both running and studying. He's determined, hardworking, and responsible, juggling schoolbooks and running shoes daily. This person has clear values and vision for what they can do.

In the 1950s, it was believed that running a mile in under four minutes was impossible. It was a huge barrier in the world of sports. But this young runner didn't let that stop him. He believed in setting goals and working hard to achieve them. Every morning, he woke up early to train, and every evening, he hit the books, studying to become a doctor. He was dedicated to each of his passions, showing how responsibility and accountability lead to great things.

This runner didn't just train harder; he trained smarter. Using his knowledge from his studies, he learned about how the human body works and used that to improve his running. He knew that being true to himself meant putting in the effort and understanding every step of his journey.

On May 6, 1954, a race on a small track changed history. The young man lined up to race. The crowd watched with bated breath as he ran, not knowing what they were about to witness. With each stride, he pushed past the limits everyone thought were unbreakable. As he crossed the finish line, the clock stopped at 3 minutes and 59.4 seconds. He had done it! He ran a mile in under four minutes, proving that with a dream and dedicated action, incredible things are possible.

But this story doesn't end there. After his amazing achievement, he didn't rest. He went on to become a respected doctor, helping countless people with his medical knowledge. He continued to show that caring about what you do and being responsible makes a big difference in the world.

This young runner, known to the world as Roger Bannister, became a symbol of what it means to break barriers. His story teaches us that setting clear goals, dedication, and genuinely caring about our actions leads to extraordinary accomplishments. Roger Bannister showed the world that we can achieve the impossible.

So, what about you? What are you passionate about? What challenges have you overcome that could inspire others? By being responsible and genuine, you, too, can make a lasting mark on the world. Your journey could be the next story of inspiration, showing that with dedication and care, can achieve the extraordinary.

Think about applying Roger's story to your own life. Start by identifying your passions and setting clear, achievable goals. Then, create a plan and hold yourself accountable for following through.

Imagine the impact you'll have on your community. Maybe you want to start a local initiative, mentor young people, or advocate for a cause you believe in. By taking action, you inspire others to do the same. Your genuine efforts create positive change far beyond what you see around you.

Commit to your passions and take responsibility for doing it. Allied, we can break through barriers and achieve remarkable things. So, take that first step. Embrace your passions, be accountable, and make your mark on the world.

What's stopping you?

What counts in life is not the mere fact
that we have lived. It is what difference we
have made to the lives of others that will
determine the significance of the life we lead.

—NELSON MANDELA

RESOURCES

AUTHORS AND EXPERTS ON ACCOUNTABILITY

Below, you'll find a list of favorite authors and experts who have written notable books and articles on personal accountability. Through their extensive research and compelling writings, they provide valuable insights and practical tools to help us better understand the importance of taking responsibility for our actions. Having a coach to guide you through the process can be incredibly beneficial on your pathway to higher accountability.

The Four-Minute Mile by **Roger Bannister** – This book provides a firsthand account of his journey to breaking the four-minute mile. It offers insights into his training, the challenges he faced, and the historic race that made him a legend.

The Five Dysfunctions of a Team by **Patrick Lencioni** uses a fable to reveal common team pitfalls and offers practical solutions. Lencioni, a leading expert in organizational health, provides strategies to build trust, encourage healthy conflict, and improve team performance.

Stephen R. Covey's *The 7 Habits of Highly Effective People* offers a Practices-centered approach to solving personal and professional problems. Covey presents seven habits that foster effectiveness, including being proactive and prioritizing important tasks. His emphasis on fairness, integrity, and continuous improvement has inspired millions worldwide.

Angela Merkel: The Authorized Biography by **Stefan Kornelius** – This comprehensive biography provides a deep dive into Merkel's personal and political life, drawing on exclusive access to her inner circle and highlighting her journey from East Germany to becoming the world's most powerful woman.

The Chancellor: The Remarkable Odyssey of Angela Merkel **by Kati Marton** – Marton paints a vivid portrait of Merkel's rise to power, her strategic acumen, and her pivotal role in global politics, offering insights into her unique leadership style and legacy.

Roger Connors, Tom Smith, and Craig Hickman, co-authors of *The Oz Principle*, which is considered a definitive guide on personal and organizational accountability. The book emphasizes the importance of taking personal ownership of one's actions to achieve the best results in any setting (PenguinRandomhouse.com).

Brené Brown – In her book *Dare to Lead: Brave Work. Tough Conversations. Whole Hearts,* Brené Brown explores the importance of vulnerability in leadership and accountability. She emphasizes the need for leaders to acknowledge their own areas of growth and cultivate a culture of openness and accountability within their teams.

LEADING BY EXAMPLE

As highlighted by Harvard Business School, leaders must exemplify ethical behavior and accountability themselves before expecting it from their teams. This involves setting clear expectations, demonstrating integrity, and being transparent about both successes and failures.

Chapter 8:
Practice Eight,
Validate and Affirm

THE SPIRITUALLY CENTERED HIGHER-LEVEL ADAPTABLE AND FLUID LEADER

ELEMENT TWO: ADAPTABLE AND FLUID ◌
ELEMENT THREE: VISIONARY AND EXPANSIVE ⇒

EMBRACE CHANGE AND ENCOURAGE OPEN COMMUNICATION, FOSTERING FLEXIBILITY AND EMPATHY

I can't recall ever hearing someone say, *"I validate and affirm your feelings."* Instead, you might hear responses like, *"I understand,"* or *"Let's focus on the issue at hand."* But how often do we truly recognize the emotions behind the words? Picture a student telling their teacher, *"I can't do this math problem. I'm just too stupid."* A common response might be, *"You're not stupid. Let's try again."* While well-meaning, this response overlooks the student's underlying frustration and self-doubt.

Now, consider if the teacher responded, *"You seem really frustrated with this problem. It's okay to feel that way. You're capable, and we can work through this together."* This simple shift acknowledges the student's emotions, validating their feelings and affirming their self-worth. The teacher doesn't just hear the words; they understand the emotion behind them.

Validating and affirming someone's feelings means recognizing their emotions and showing them that their feelings are legitimate. It's about seeing the person behind the words and uplifting their self-worth. When we practice validation and affirmation, we create an environment where people feel understood, respected, and valued.

Take the example of a team member who's upset about a project deadline. Instead of saying, *"We all have deadlines to meet, just get it done,"* a validating higher-level leader might say, *"You seem really stressed about this deadline. It's completely normal to feel overwhelmed. Your feelings are important, and I believe in your ability to handle this. How can we support you?"* This approach doesn't just address the task at hand but also acknowledges the person's emotional experience, showing empathy and support.

In another instance, consider a friend who says, *"I'm so anxious about this presentation. I always mess up."* Instead of responding with, *"You'll be fine, just relax,"* an affirming response would be, *"It's normal to feel anxious about presentations. Your feelings are valid. Remember, you've prepared well and have the skills to do a great job. I believe in you."* This response validates their anxiety and affirms their abilities, boosting their confidence.

By focusing on validation and affirmation, we greatly improve our interactions with others. We create a safe space where people feel comfortable expressing their emotions, which leads to stronger relationships and increased trust. When people feel validated and affirmed, they are more likely to be open, honest, and engaged.

My boss, Walter, the regional sales manager at the music distribution company where I worked many years ago, was great at validating and affirming his employees. I was very young back then and didn't realize what he was doing. When I was upset or frustrated about something, Walter could see what was happening with me, and his empathy and compassion would come alive. As it turns out, many of my co-workers had similar experiences with him.

I even once talked with his counterpart Dennis about what a good boss I thought Walter was. It was an unforgettable conversation.

"Dennis," I said, *"You know that I think Walter is a great boss. I've got to tell you about this one time Walter called me into his office. I could tell right away something was up. It turns out he heard about the confrontation I had with a co-worker. You know how Walter is—*

he listened and then told me he understood where I was coming from."

Dennis nodded, saying, "*Oh yeah, Walter's great at that.*"

"*Exactly! So, he shared this story about how he once had a co-worker who was just a total screw-up. Walter and the team had to keep covering for the guy's mistakes, and it was really getting to him. He even vented to a mentor about it, and the mentor told him he should talk to the guy and see what's going on.*"

"*Sure, that sounds like Walter. Always trying to understand people,*" Dennis agreed.

"*Right, so Walter went and talked to this guy and found out what was bothering him, and after that conversation, the guy stopped screwing up all the time, and they became good friends. Walter said he was really glad he made the effort.*"

Dennis paused for a moment and then said, "*I was the screw-up.*"

"*What? Really?*" I asked, surprised.

"*Yeah, that guy was me,*" Dennis said with a wry smile. "*I've always been grateful that Walter reached out to me instead of just writing me off. That conversation was a turning point in my life.*"

We can never tell how much of an impact we have on others' lives if we don't put our ego aside and understand what the other person is going through. Others want the same things that we want deep down, but sometimes in the heat of the moment, harsh words mask the little boy or little girl inside us.

TURNING TOUGH TALKS INTO REMARKABLE ENCOUNTERS

Conversations involving emotions like sadness, discouragement, and frustration often require a gentle touch, but what about those moments when anger and other intense negative emotions come into play? It's easy for these conversations to spiral into conflict, leaving both parties feeling hurt and misunderstood. However, by focusing on validating and affirming, even these heated interactions can be turned into remarkable encounters. When we acknowledge someone's anger and the reasons behind it, we make an opportunity for deeper understanding and resolution. For example, if a team member lashes out in a meeting, a higher-level leader who validates their feelings might say, *"I can see you're really angry about this decision. Your feelings are valid, and I want to understand more about what's upsetting you."*

In these intense moments, it's crucial to listen beyond the anger to the underlying emotions driving it. Anger is often a mask for deeper feelings like fear, hurt, frustration, feeling disrespected, trapped, forced, or pressured into something. By validating these emotions and affirming the person's right to feel them, we defuse the immediate tension and pave the way for constructive dialogue. Instead of responding defensively or dismissively, try saying, *"It sounds like you're feeling disrespected and maybe even hurt by what's happened. Let's talk about what we can do to address this."* Using this approach shows empathy and encourages the other person to open up, leading to a more meaningful and productive conversation. By turning conflicts into opportunities for connection and clarification, we can flip even the most challenging interactions into remarkable encounters.

Walter successfully used this same approach with Dennis a few times early in their friendship. He validated Dennis's feelings without necessarily agreeing with his point of view. This is an important thing that I didn't understand at first. I thought that validating and affirming someone might give the impression that I agreed with them, but I was wrong. You might be thinking, as I did, that validating and affirming could make you look weak or feel like you have lost an argument. For me, the shift in perspective came when I focused on the desired outcome. If my goal was to win an argument, then acknowledging the other person's feelings seemed impossible. But if my goal was to de-escalate the situation, my mindset shifted to validating and affirming.

Is it always possible to choose the higher-level mindset of being open, empathetic, and flexible? Probably not. I don't think anyone can bring their "A" game *all the time.*

> Unfortunately, civility is hard to codify or legislate, but you know it when you see it. It's possible to disagree without being disagreeable.
>
> —SANDRA DAY O'CONNOR

FREE TOUGH TALKS CHEAT SHEET: 5 STEPS TO BETTER CONVERSATIONS

Ever find yourself walking into a conversation, and within minutes, it's a full-blown argument? You didn't intend to start a conflict, but suddenly, you're stuck in a back-and-forth that's going nowhere. Maybe you've been misunderstood, or maybe emotions are running high, and there seems to be no way out without someone getting hurt or defensive.

It's frustrating, right? You try to stay calm, but the situation keeps escalating, and before you know it, you're both locked in an emotional tug-of-war. You want to communicate better, but every attempt just seems to make things worse. It's exhausting and leaves you feeling defeated, questioning what went wrong.

The good news is that conversations don't have to be this hard. Imagine having a quick, go-to guide to keep things calm, productive, and grounded—no matter how tense things get. That's what the **FREE Tough Talks Cheat Sheet** does. It equips you with five simple yet powerful steps that will help you stay in control, recognize emotions, and focus on finding common ground.

Stop letting difficult conversations drain your energy. With these five easy-to-follow steps, you'll approach every conversation with confidence, knowing how to connect, validate, and resolve conflicts smoothly.

bit.ly/toughtalksmadeeasy

WHY WE STRUGGLE TO VALIDATE OR AFFIRM OTHERS

We struggle to validate or affirm someone's feelings for several reasons. I'll address some of today's hot topics that divide us. Politics can be a major stumbling block. When someone holds different political views, it's hard to look past the disagreement and recognize their emotions. For example, if a friend is angry about a political issue you disagree with, you might find it difficult to validate them without feeling like you're endorsing their viewpoint.

Belonging to a group with opposing views can also make it tough to validate someone. In the workplace, if your team is split over a new policy, you might hesitate to affirm the frustrations of a colleague who supports a stance you oppose. You may fear that doing so will make you seem disloyal to your group.

Religious differences and varying belief systems also pose challenges. If someone shares their emotional struggle related to a belief that contradicts your own, validating their feelings might seem like you're betraying your own values. For example, if someone feels hurt because their religious beliefs are not being respected, but those beliefs clash with your own, it is difficult to empathize without feeling like you're betraying your faith.

In all these situations, the fear of appearing weak, disloyal, or inconsistent with our beliefs stops us from truly validating and affirming others.

SHIFTING OUR MINDSET TO VALIDATE AND AFFIRM

Despite the challenges, it's possible to shift our mindset to validate and affirm others, even when facing differing views or beliefs. The key is to **focus on the person's emotions rather than their opinions**. For instance, in a political disagreement, instead of debating the issue, you might say, *"I see this topic makes you really upset. Your* *feelings are valid."* This way, you acknowledge their emotions without having to agree with their viewpoint.

On the other hand, a less productive approach might be reacting defensively or trying to immediately counter their opinion. For example, if you respond with, "I don't understand why you're so upset about this," it dismisses their feelings and will likely escalate the tension. This not only shuts down open communication but also makes the person feel invalidated, turning the conversation into a combative debate rather than a supportive exchange.

In group settings with opposing views, **separate the person from the position they hold**. For example, if a colleague is frustrated about a new policy you disagree with, you might say, *"I understand that this policy is causing you stress. It's important to feel heard."* This approach helps maintain support without compromising your own stance.

When it comes to religious differences, it's helpful to remember that validating someone's feelings **does not mean you agree with their beliefs.** If someone feels hurt because their religious practices are not respected, you could respond with, *"I see that this is really important to you, and it's causing you pain. Your feelings matter."* This way, you show empathy and respect for their emotions without betraying your own beliefs.

By focusing on the other person's emotional experience, we find common ground. This mindset shift allows us to connect on a human level, even when our opinions differ. Practicing active listening and showing genuine interest in how the other person feels helps to bridge the gap created by differing views.

For instance, if a friend is upset about a community issue that you see differently, you might say, *"I see that this is really important to you, and it's causing you a lot of distress. Let's talk more about why you feel this way."* This opens up a space for understanding and connection rather than conflict.

Shifting our mindset to validate and affirm requires effort and practice. It's about being open, empathetic, and willing to see the person behind the opinion. This approach not only improves our interactions but also fosters compassion and understanding.

LEARNING TO VALIDATE AND AFFIRM

The techniques for validating and affirming another person in difficult conversations take learning and practice. Recognizing and using these techniques also requires a shift in how we approach our interactions. It's not easy, but with effort, it becomes more natural over time.

To start, **focus on active listening**. This means giving your full attention to the person speaking without planning your response while they're talking. For example, during a heated meeting with my cycling team, tensions were high because of a major race that was fast approaching. People were frustrated and stressed, and communication was breaking down. One of my teammates, Josh, was especially vocal. He was upset about the training schedule and felt that the workload was unfairly distributed. As he spoke, it was clear that his words were fueled by more than just professional concerns—a lot of personal frustration and stress came through.

Instead of responding defensively or trying to immediately counter his points, I decided to use the techniques of addressing emotions, not just words. I started by really **paying attention** to Josh, making eye contact as he spoke, and showing through my body language that I was fully present and listening. When Josh paused, I reflected on what I heard back to him to show him that I wanted to understand. *"It sounds like you're feeling overwhelmed by the* *training schedule and frustrated with how things are being handled."* This simple act of acknowledging his feelings seemed to defuse some of his anger. He nodded and continued to share more about what was bothering him.

Next, **practice empathy** by trying to see the situation from the other person's perspective. Imagine how you would feel if you were in their shoes. This helps you to understand their emotions better. For instance, I tried to **"read minds"** a bit by suggesting, *"It seems like you're also feeling worried about how this training might impact your performance in the upcoming race. Is that right?"* Josh looked relieved that someone had picked up on this underlying concern. He admitted that he was indeed worried about balancing this intense training with his performance goals.

Here's another helpful technique: Instead of saying, *"You're overreacting,"* try saying, *"This is making you really upset."* This way, you express understanding without judgment, making the other person feel heard and respected. To show that I **truly understood,** I added, *"Given everything on your plate, it makes sense that you're feeling this way. Anyone would find this situation challenging."* This validation helped Josh feel that his emotions were normal and justified.

It's also important to avoid minimizing feelings. Phrases like *"It's not a big deal"* or *"You'll get over it"* will make someone feel dismissed. Instead, validate their experience by saying, *"I understand that this is important to you. Your feelings are valid."* Throughout our conversation, I made sure to **treat Josh as an equal**, reacting naturally to his emotions and showing compassion without patronizing him. I used validating statements like, *"I'm here for you,"* and *"That must have been really tough,"* which helped Josh feel supported and understood.

Practice makes perfect, and the more you use these techniques, the better you'll become at validating and affirming others. Start with small, everyday interactions and gradually apply these skills to more challenging conversations. The goal is to build trust and understanding, making each interaction more positive and productive.

You never really understand a person until you consider things from his point of view.

—HARPER LEE

GUIDE TO ADDRESSING EMOTIONS, NOT JUST WORDS, IN CONFLICT

When conflicts arise, it's important to address not only the words being spoken but also the emotions behind them. Here's a practical guide to help you navigate these tricky conversations and validate feelings effectively.

1. Recall Emotions

Goal: *Build awareness of different emotions and understand how they manifest in various scenarios.*

Activity:

- **Identify Emotions:** Start by listing common emotions (e.g., happy, sad, angry, scared, surprised). Practice recognizing these emotions in different scenarios.

- **Recall Situations:** Think of past conflicts. Recall what emotions were involved and how they were expressed.

Reflective Exercise:

Journaling: Write about a recent conflict and list the emotions you experienced. How did you recognize these emotions? What triggered them?

Ask Yourself

"Remember a time you felt really upset? What were the emotions you experienced? Anger? Frustration?"

Example:

"Let's say you had a conflict with a family member. You might have felt anger because you believed you were disrespected, sadness because of the strain in the relationship and the stress of the rest of your family, and helplessness because you couldn't resolve things. Try listing those emotions—anger, sadness, helplessness, and perhaps even guilt."

2. Explain Emotions

Goal: *Develop the ability to articulate and understand emotional experiences.*

Activity:

- **Describe Emotions:** Use simple language to describe what each emotion feels like. For instance, "Anger feels like a burning sensation in my chest."

- **Discuss Scenarios:** Talk about different scenarios and how they might make someone feel.

Reflective Exercise:

Emotional Mapping: Create a map of different emotions and write descriptions for each. Reflect on how these emotions have appeared in your interactions.

Ask Yourself:

What does anger feel like to me? How does my body feel when I am happy? How is that different from when I am scared?

Example:

"Imagine your friend forgot your birthday. How would that make you feel? Maybe sad or even angry?"

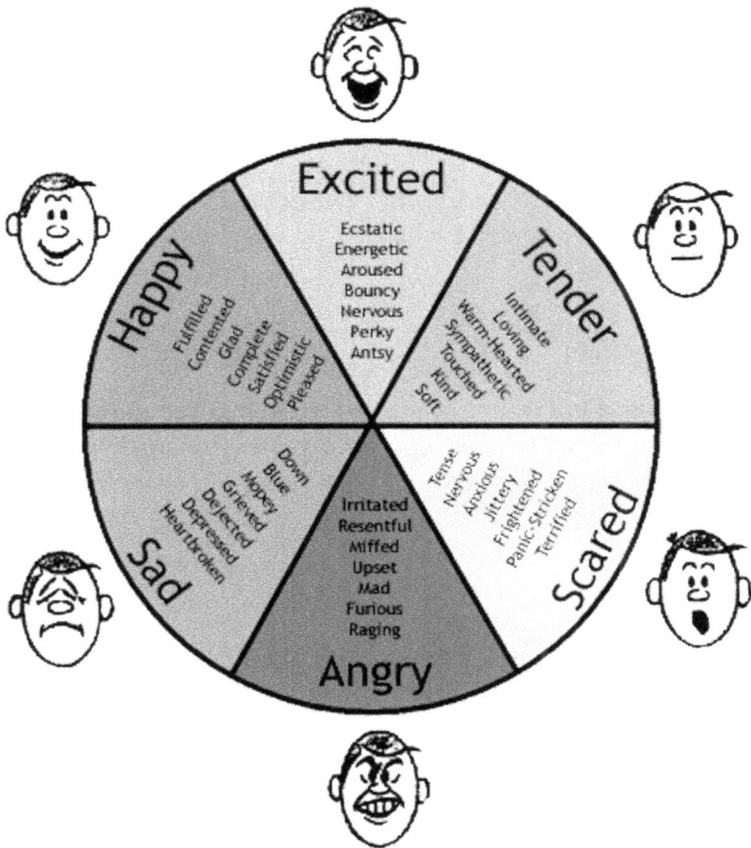

3. Use Emotional Knowledge

Goal: *Apply understanding of emotions to improve interactions and resolve conflicts.*

Activity:

- **Role-Playing:** Act out different conflict scenarios and practice identifying and addressing emotions.

- **Practice Responses:** Practice what you would say in these situations to validate the other person's feelings.

Reflective Exercise:

Self-Assessment: After role-playing, reflect on what you did well and what could be improved. Write down specific instances where you successfully validated and affirmed emotions.

Ask Yourself:

Do I honestly think this conflict was caused by hostility and malice or was it because of an accident or confusion? Did the other person intend to hurt and upset me?

Example:

"Let's role-play. I'll be the friend who forgot your birthday, and you express how you feel. Then, let's practice a response like, 'You're really upset because I forgot your birthday. That's totally understandable.'"

4. Analyze Emotional Triggers

Goal: *Understand the root causes of emotional reactions and how to manage them.*

Activity:

- **Discuss Triggers:** Identify what events or actions trigger certain emotions.

- **Explore Reactions:** Talk about how different people might react to the same situation.

Reflective Exercise:

Trigger Diary: Keep a diary of situations that trigger strong emotions. Reflect on why these triggers affect you and how you can manage your reactions.

Ask Yourself:

What makes me feel anxious? Is it something like public speaking or a big test coming up? Is there something that always makes me want to lash out? What kinds of triggers do I have and how do I usually react to them?

Example:

Trigger: Being interrupted during a conversation.

Reaction: One person might feel frustrated and lash out, while another could shut down and withdraw, feeling disrespected but choosing to stay silent.

Trigger: Being criticized in front of others.

Reaction: Some people might react with embarrassment and attempt to defend themselves, while others could feel shame and retreat into themselves, avoiding further interaction.

5. Evaluate Responses

Goal: *Identify and refine effective strategies for emotional regulation and conflict resolution.*

Activity:

- **Compare Reactions**: Discuss different ways of responding to emotional situations and evaluate which are more effective.

- **Reflect on Outcomes:** Consider past conflicts and how different responses might have changed the outcome.

Reflective Exercise:

Outcome Analysis: Write about a past conflict and the outcome. Reflect on how a different approach could have altered the result. What strategies would you use next time?

Ask Yourself:

How do I usually respond when I am involved in a disagreement? Are my responses effective? Do they get me what I want? What could I do differently?

Example:

Conflict: A disagreement with a friend over political views.

Reflection: I could have focused on understanding their perspective instead of trying to win the argument. This might have led to a more respectful conversation and preserved the friendship despite our differences.

6. Create Strategies

Goal: *Prepare for future conflicts by creating effective emotional management and communication strategies.*

Activity:

- **Plan Ahead:** Create a list of go-to phrases that validate emotions (e.g., *"You're upset," "You're angry," "I understand why you're feeling this way," "That sounds really tough."*).

- **Write Scenarios:** Write out potential conflict scenarios and plan how to address the emotions involved.

Reflective Exercise:

Strategy Review: Regularly review and update your list of validating phrases and scenarios. Reflect on how these strategies have helped in real conflicts.

Ask Yourself:

What have people said to me that has made me feel heard or understood when I have been frustrated? What words or tones were used that helped me feel comfortable?

Example:

Scenario: A friend is angry after an argument with someone else.

Go-to Phrase: "It sounds like that really got under your skin. I can imagine how frustrating that must have been."

Create a cheat sheet of phrases. For example, *'I get why you're frustrated,'* and *'It sounds like you're really disappointed.'* Keep this handy for when conflicts arise.

By following this guide, you'll be better equipped to handle conflicts by addressing the emotions involved, ensuring that everyone feels heard and validated. Practice makes real progress, so keep these strategies in mind and use them whenever conflicts arise.

ADDRESSING EMOTIONS, NOT JUST WORDS: PRACTICAL SCENARIOS FOR EVERYDAY LIFE

Conflicts are a part of life, whether they occur at work, within families, or among friends. Often, these conflicts arise not from the actual words spoken but from the emotions driving those words. Addressing emotions, not just words, is a powerful technique that transforms heated exchanges into opportunities for understanding and growth. This approach involves recognizing and validating the feelings behind the words, creating a space where empathy and real communication flourish.

In the following scenarios, we'll meet some new people and see how this technique works in different situations. Whether it's between coworkers like Sarah and Tom, friends on opposite ends of the political spectrum like Jane and Mike, individuals with differing religious views like Emily and Lisa, or a parent and child like Laura and Frankie, the practice of addressing emotions, not just words, remains the same. These narratives will illustrate how focusing on feelings leads to deeper understanding and effective conflict resolution, fostering stronger and more compassionate relationships.

Empathy is choosing to see ourselves in another despite our differences. It's recognizing that the same humanity—the same desire for meaning, fulfillment, and security—exists in each of us, even if it's expressed uniquely.

—DR. VIVEK MURTHY

ADDRESSING EMOTIONS, NOT JUST WORDS: SARAH AND TOM, WORKPLACE CONFLICT SCENARIO

Workplace conflicts happen all the time. Different personalities, high-stress situations, and tight deadlines create a perfect storm for misunderstandings and disagreements. But by addressing emotions, not just words, we transform these conflicts into opportunities for growth and collaboration. This method helps in recognizing and validating the underlying feelings driving the conversation, leading to more empathetic and productive discussions. *Allied We Can …* accomplish amazing things when we understand and support each other.

Sarah and Tom always worked well together, but lately, things were tense. A big project deadline was approaching, and the stress was taking its toll. One morning, the tension boiled over.

Tom, looking frustrated, stormed over to Sarah's desk. *"Sarah, I can't believe you missed the meeting yesterday! We needed your input, and now we're behind schedule!"*

Sarah, already frazzled, shot back, *"I had an emergency to deal with, Tom! It's not like I missed it on purpose. You're always blaming me when things go wrong!"*

The office fell silent as their colleagues watched the confrontation. Feeling the tension escalate, Sarah took a step back and remembered the techniques she had recently learned about addressing emotions, not just words.

Taking a deep breath, Sarah made eye contact with Tom and said, *"Tom, I see you're really upset right now. It sounds like you're feeling overwhelmed by the project deadline and frustrated because my absence has put us behind. Is that right?"*

Tom, still visibly upset, nodded. *"Yes, exactly. We're already behind and missing that meeting didn't help at all."*

Sarah continued, *"I understand why you're feeling this way. I didn't want to miss the meeting either. I had an emergency that couldn't wait, and I'm really sorry it affected the project."*

Tom's posture softened slightly as he felt his emotions acknowledged. Sarah then tried to address the deeper concern. *"It seems like you're also worried about how we're going to meet the deadline now. Is that correct?"*

Tom sighed, some of the tension leaving his shoulders. *"Yeah, I'm really worried about that. We've put so much effort into this project, and I don't want it to fail."*

Sarah nodded, showing she understood. *"I get that. Given everything on our plate, it makes sense that you're feeling stressed. How about we come up with a plan to get back on track together?"*

By acknowledging Tom's emotions without necessarily agreeing with his point of view, Sarah created a space for real understanding. She wasn't taking sides; she was validating his feelings.

"Let's focus on solutions," Sarah suggested. *"What if we reschedule the meeting from today and go over everything we missed? I will also stay late this week to help catch up. Does that sound like a good start?"*

Tom, feeling heard and understood, agreed. *"Yes, that sounds like a good plan. Thanks, Sarah."*

As they worked together to reschedule the meeting and adjust their workload, the atmosphere between them improved. They moved from a place of confrontation to one of collaboration, finding ways to support each other better.

Reflective Exercise:

- Think of a recent conflict you experienced at work or in your personal life. Identify the emotions involved for both yourself and the other person.

- How did you address these emotions during the conflict? What techniques did you use, and how effective were they?

- Reflect on how you could apply the validation and affirmation techniques demonstrated by Sarah in your own situation. Write down specific phrases or actions you would use.

Highlighted Techniques:

- **Active Listening:** Making eye contact and showing through body language that you are fully present.

- **Validating Emotions:** Acknowledging the other person's feelings without necessarily agreeing with their viewpoint.

- **Affirming Statements:** Using phrases that show you understand and respect the other person's emotions.

- **Solution-Oriented Approach:** Proposing actionable steps to address the issue and move forward.

Discussion on the Outcome:

By validating and affirming Tom's emotions, Sarah was able to de-escalate the situation and shift the focus to finding a solution. This approach not only resolved the immediate conflict but also strengthened their working relationship, creating a more supportive and collaborative environment.

ADDRESSING EMOTIONS, NOT JUST WORDS: JANE AND MIKE, POLITICAL CONFLICT SCENARIO

Political discussions can be some of the most heated, especially when individuals hold strong opposing views. In this scenario, we'll see how two coworkers, Jane and Mike, handle their political differences by addressing emotions, not just words. This narrative will illustrate the technique and show how it leads to better understanding and respect.

Jane and Mike worked together at the same company but were on opposite ends of the political spectrum. Jane leaned liberal, while Mike was conservative. Their political discussions often turned into heated arguments, leaving both of them frustrated and upset.

One day, during a break, the topic of immigration policy came up. Mike passionately argued for stricter immigration laws, while Jane supported more inclusive policies. The conversation quickly escalated.

Mike, with a raised voice, said, *"How can you support open borders? It's dangerous and irresponsible!"*

Jane, remaining calm, responded, *"Mike, I believe in strong immigration laws, but I also think we need to be compassionate and fair. We should find a balance."*

Their coworkers watched uncomfortably, sensing the growing tension. Jane decided to take a different approach this time. Remembering a workshop on addressing emotions, not just words, she decided to apply what she had learned.

Taking a deep breath, Jane made eye contact with Mike and said, *"Mike, I see you're really upset about this issue. It sounds like you're worried about the safety and security of our country. Is that right?"*

Mike, still frustrated but slightly taken aback by Jane's calm response, nodded. *"Yes, exactly. I just think it's unfair to let people in without strict checks."*

Jane continued, *"I understand why you feel that way. It's a huge issue, and it's really important to you. I also want our country to be safe, but I believe in a different approach. It seems like we both care about the same goal but see different ways to achieve it. Does that sound accurate?"*

Mike, feeling his emotions being acknowledged, softened his tone. *"Yes, that makes sense. I didn't realize you cared about security, too."*

Jane added, *"Given our different experiences and backgrounds, it makes sense that we'd have different perspectives on the best way to achieve this. I appreciate hearing your side, and I hope you understand mine too."*

By acknowledging Mike's emotions and validating his feelings without necessarily agreeing with his point of view, Jane created a space for real understanding. She wasn't taking sides; she was simply recognizing the emotions driving their words.

Mike, feeling heard and respected, responded more calmly. *"I see where you're coming from, Jane. Maybe we can find some common ground or at least understand each other better."*

As their conversation continued, the atmosphere shifted from confrontation to mutual respect. They didn't completely agree on the issue, but they were able to discuss it more constructively and find areas where they could agree, like the importance of balancing safety and compassion.

By addressing the emotions behind the words, Jane transformed a potentially divisive argument into a productive dialogue. This scenario highlights how focusing on feelings leads to deeper understanding and more effective conflict resolution, even when discussing contentious issues. *Allied We Can…* find common ground and respect, even across political divides.

Reflective Exercise:

- Think of a recent political or contentious discussion you experienced at work or in your personal life. Identify the emotions involved for both yourself and the other person.

- How did you address these emotions during the discussion? What techniques did you use, and how effective were they?

- Reflect on how you could apply the validation and affirmation techniques demonstrated by Jane in your own situation. Write down specific phrases or actions you would use.

Highlighted Techniques:

- **Active Listening:** Making eye contact and showing through body language that you're fully present.

- **Validating Emotions**: Acknowledging the other person's feelings without necessarily agreeing with their viewpoint.

- **Affirming Statements:** Using phrases that show you understand and respect the other person's emotions.

- **Common Goals:** Highlighting shared concerns or objectives to build a foundation for mutual understanding.

Discussion on the Outcome:

By validating and affirming Mike's emotions, Jane was able to de-escalate the situation and shift the focus to finding common ground. This approach not only resolved the immediate conflict but also strengthened their working relationship, creating a more respectful and collaborative environment.

ADDRESSING EMOTIONS, NOT JUST WORDS: EMILY AND LISA, RELIGIOUS CONFLICT SCENARIO

Religious discussions are some of the most sensitive conversations, especially when individuals hold strong opposing views. In this scenario, we'll see how two coworkers, Emily and Lisa, handle their religious differences by addressing emotions, not just words. This narrative will illustrate the technique and show how it leads to better understanding and respect.

Emily and Lisa worked together at the same nonprofit organization but were on opposite ends of the religious spectrum. Emily was conservative in her beliefs, while Lisa held more liberal views. Their discussions about their religious beliefs often turned into heated arguments, leaving both of them offended and angry.

One day, during a lunch break, the topic of religious inclusivity in their organization came up. Emily argued for maintaining traditional practices, while Lisa supported more inclusive approaches. The conversation quickly escalated.

With a raised voice, Emily said, *"How can you support changing our traditions? It's disrespectful to our faith!"*

Lisa, remaining calm, responded, *"Emily, I believe in respecting our traditions, but I also think we need to be more inclusive and welcoming to everyone. We should find a balance."*

Their coworkers watched uncomfortably, sensing the growing tension. Lisa decided to take a different approach this time. Remembering a workshop on addressing emotions, not just words, she decided to apply what she had learned.

Taking a deep breath, Lisa made eye contact with Emily and said, *"Emily, I see you're really upset about this issue. It sounds like you're worried that changing our traditions might undermine our faith. Is that right?"*

Emily, still visibly upset, nodded. *"Yes, exactly. Our traditions are important, and changing them feels wrong."*

Lisa continued, *"I understand why you feel that way. It's a huge issue, and it's really important to you. I also value our traditions but believe a different approach might be better for inclusivity. It seems like we both care about the same goal but see different ways to achieve it. Does that sound accurate?"*

Emily, feeling her emotions being acknowledged, softened her tone. *"Yes, that makes sense. I didn't realize you cared about traditions too."*

Lisa added, *"Given our different experiences and backgrounds, it makes sense that we'd have different perspectives on the best way to achieve this. I appreciate hearing your side, and I hope you understand mine too."*

By acknowledging Emily's emotions and validating her feelings without necessarily agreeing with her point of view, Lisa created a space for real understanding. She wasn't taking sides; she was simply recognizing the emotions driving their words.

Emily, feeling heard and respected, responded more calmly. *"I see where you're coming from, Lisa. Maybe we can find some common ground or at least understand each other better."*

As their conversation continued, the atmosphere shifted from one of confrontation to one of mutual respect. They didn't completely agree on the issue, but they were able to discuss it more constructively and find areas where they agreed, like the importance of balancing tradition and inclusivity.

Lisa transformed a potentially divisive argument into a productive dialogue by addressing the emotions behind the words. This scenario highlights how focusing on feelings leads to deeper understanding and more effective conflict resolution, even when discussing contentious issues.

Reflective Exercise:

- Think of a recent religious or sensitive discussion you experienced at work or in your personal life. Identify the emotions involved for both yourself and the other person.

- How did you address these emotions during the discussion? What techniques did you use, and how effective were they?

- Reflect on how you could apply the validation and affirmation techniques demonstrated by Lisa in your own situation. Write down specific phrases or actions you would use.

Highlighted Techniques:

- **Active Listening:** Making eye contact and showing through body language that you're fully present.

- **Validating Emotions:** Acknowledging the other person's feelings without necessarily agreeing with their viewpoint.

- **Affirming Statements:** Using phrases that show you understand and respect the other person's emotions.

- **Common Goals:** Highlighting shared concerns or objectives to build a foundation for mutual understanding.

Discussion on the Outcome:

By validating and affirming Emily's emotions, Lisa was able to de-escalate the situation and shift the focus to finding common ground. This approach not only resolved the immediate conflict but also strengthened their working relationship, creating a more respectful and collaborative environment.

ADDRESSING EMOTIONS, NOT JUST WORDS: A PARENT-CHILD CONFLICT SCENARIO

Parenting is challenging, especially when dealing with conflicts with children. In this scenario, we'll see how a mom, Laura, handles an issue with her teenage son, Frankie, by addressing emotions, not just words. This narrative will illustrate the technique and show how it leads to better understanding and a stronger relationship.

Laura had a good relationship with her teenage son, Frankie, but lately, things had been tense. Frankie was spending more time out with friends and less time on his schoolwork. One evening, Laura noticed that Frankie had missed another homework assignment, and she decided to confront him about it.

Laura, feeling frustrated, approached Frankie's room and knocked on the door. *"Frankie, we need to talk,"* she said, her voice firm.

Frankie, already irritated, responded, *"What now, Mom? I'm busy."*

Laura took a deep breath, remembering the techniques she had learned about addressing emotions, not just words. Instead of reacting to Frankie's attitude, she decided to focus on his feelings.

"Frankie, I see you're upset," Laura began, making eye contact with her son. *"It sounds like you're feeling overwhelmed with everything going on. Is that right?"*

Frankie, still defensive, shrugged. *"Yeah, I guess. There's just a lot happening right now."*

Laura continued, *"I understand why you're feeling this way. School, friends, and everything else is a lot to handle. I'm worried because I've noticed you've missed a few homework assignments, and I want to make sure you're doing okay. will you tell me what's been going on?"*

Frankie sighed, some of the tension leaving his body. *"I've been trying to keep up, but it feels like too much sometimes. And I just want to hang out with my friends and relax."*

Laura nodded, showing she understood. *"It makes sense that you're feeling stressed. Balancing school and social life isn't easy. I'm here to help you figure it out. What can we do to make things easier for you?"*

By acknowledging Frankie's emotions and validating his feelings without necessarily agreeing with his behavior, Laura created a space for real understanding. She wasn't taking sides but simply recognizing the emotions driving his actions.

Frankie, feeling heard and respected, responded more calmly. *"Maybe we can set up a schedule that gives me some time to hang out with my friends but also get my homework done. I just need some help organizing everything."*

Laura smiled, relieved that they were finding common ground. *"That sounds like a great idea. Let's sit down together and come up with a plan. I'm here to support you, Frankie."*

As they worked together to create a balanced schedule, the atmosphere between them improved. They moved from a place of confrontation to one of collaboration, de-escalating the situation.

By addressing the emotions behind the words, Laura transformed a potentially destructive confrontation into a productive and empathetic dialogue. This scenario highlights how focusing on feelings leads to deeper understanding and effective conflict resolution, creating a stronger and more compassionate relationship between parent and child.

Reflective Exercise:

- Think of a recent conflict you experienced with your child. Identify the emotions involved for both yourself and your child.

- How did you address these emotions during the conflict? What techniques did you use, and how effective were they?

- Reflect on how you could apply the validation and affirmation techniques demonstrated by Laura in your own situation. Write down specific phrases or actions you would use.

Highlighted Techniques:

- **Active Listening:** Making eye contact and showing through body language that you're fully present.

- **Validating Emotions:** Acknowledging the other person's feelings without necessarily agreeing with their behavior.

- **Affirming Statements:** Using phrases that show you understand and respect the other person's emotions.

- **Common Goals:** Highlighting shared concerns or objectives to build a foundation for mutual understanding.

Discussion on the Outcome:

By validating and affirming Frankie's emotions, Laura was able to de-escalate the situation and shift the focus to finding common ground. This approach not only resolved the immediate conflict but also strengthened their relationship, creating a more supportive and collaborative environment.

A NOTE ON ARGUMENTS AND OPINIONS

People can take sides and argue over *anything*, making *any* conversation potentially messy. *Who was the best actor to play Batman? What is the worst rock album of all time? What was the most exciting year for baseball? Did Lee Harvey Oswald act alone? Should we observe Daylight Saving Time? Cats or dogs? Summer or winter? Ebooks or physical books?*

You get what I am saying. Opinions are rampant, and people are passionate, so there are endless opportunities to practice these techniques!

WRAPPING IT UP:
BRIDGING GAPS WITH WORDS, WITS, AND MARTIAN TALES

On October 17, a calm evening turned crazy when breaking news interrupted CNN's regular programming. Jake Tapper reported explosions on Mars and a Martian spaceship crash-landed in Grovers Mill, New Jersey. Witnesses described a creepy alien with a deadly heat ray, sparking widespread fear and chaos.

More Martian ships landed on Earth, their giant machines causing havoc nationwide. Cities were evacuated, and people fled in terror. In the chaos, some people started looting, others tragically committed suicide out of fear, and there were even reports of murders of people who appeared to be Martian-like. The Army's attempt to fight back was futile against the advanced alien technology.

In New York City, things got really bad as Martian machines destroyed the Empire State Building and the Chrysler Building. The air was filled with destruction and panic. Reporters, despite their fear, continued their coverage. Just when it seemed all hope was lost, reports came in that the Martians were falling ill, and their machines were grinding to a halt.

Scientists figured out that Earth's bacteria were killing the Martians. These tiny organisms, harmless to humans, were lethal to the invaders. The once unstoppable Martians were defeated by Earth's smallest life forms. People began to emerge from hiding, ready to rebuild. The broadcast ended with a hopeful message, celebrating humanity's resilience even in the face of unimaginable fear and loss.

Sounds unbelievable? Well, I made the whole thing up. The story was an adaptation of Orson Welles' legendary "War of the Worlds" broadcast, a 1938 radio show. Back then, nationwide newspapers, including *The New York Times,* ran a misinformation campaign to discredit radio, which was the hot new media of the day, and increase newspaper sales in Depression-era America. They made up stories of suicides and mass hysteria to make the event seem more dramatic.

Like in 1938, today's disinformation campaigns are causing a lot of problems in our society. These movements spread false information on purpose, especially on social media, making it difficult for people to know what's true and what's not. This kind of fake news leads to a lot of fear and hatred between different groups of people.

Disinformation spreads easily because it plays on our emotions and existing beliefs. When people see news that makes them feel angry or scared or that reinforces what they already think, they're more likely to believe it and share it with others, making fake news go viral quickly.

The effects of disinformation cause real-world problems. When people believe false stories, it preys on their biggest fears about opposing groups, often resulting in violence and even insurrections.

"A house divided against itself cannot stand," said Abraham Lincoln in 1858. When one group is the *"right group"* and another group is the *"wrong group,"* it becomes almost impossible to discuss controversial issues. The idea that we, the people, are a nation of multiple beliefs, ethnicities, and individual viewpoints creates fertile ground for debating topics and solving complex issues. When we're allied in a common cause, we find common ground to truly make America great again.

I believe this chapter is so important because it discusses communication methods to help people get past the harsh and sometimes hateful words being spewed and look at *why* someone feels the way they do without taking it personally when it's an opposing viewpoint.

I know I may sound Pollyannish; I'm aware of the deeper issues in play. The elements of spiritually centered practices that I've illustrated in earlier chapters—self-awareness, mindfulness, vulnerability, compassion, forgiveness, genuineness, and accountability—go back to the beginning of time. Talking about them in this way may seem outdated or old-fashioned to some. But the results of the higher-level leaders in my examples throughout the book illustrate their effectiveness.

By adopting these spiritually-centered practices and incorporating the techniques of validation and affirmation into our daily interactions, we begin to counteract the divisive effects of disinformation. Each conversation becomes an opportunity to build bridges rather than walls, encouraging understanding and respect even in the face of disagreement. As we strive to see beyond the surface and connect with the emotions behind the words, we cultivate a compassionate and united society. It's through these small, consistent efforts that we make meaningful change, one conversation at a time. Let's commit to this journey together, knowing that the path to a better world starts with how we communicate and connect with each other.

RESOURCES

AUTHORS AND EXPERTS ON DE-ESCALATION AND COMMUNICATION

Douglas E. Noll, a renowned mediator and author, wrote *De-Escalate: How to Calm an Angry Person in 90 Seconds or Less.* This book offers practical, neuroscience-based techniques for defusing anger and promoting peace quickly and effectively. Noll's methods are rooted in empathy and his extensive mediation experience, making his insights invaluable for handling high-stress situations

Amanda Ripley, author of *High Conflict: Why We Get Trapped and How We Get Out,* explores how deeply divisive disputes arise and how to escape the cycle of high conflict. She provides strategies to bridge differences and find common ground by examining real-world examples and scientific research.

Victoria Medvec's *Negotiate Without Fear: Strategies and Tools to Maximize Your Outcomes* offers practical tools for negotiation, focusing on boosting confidence and defining clear objectives. Her strategies are designed to help in both professional and personal conflicts, making it an essential read for effective communication and resolution.

Marshall Rosenberg – Founder of Nonviolent Communication (NVC), Marshall Rosenberg developed a communication process that emphasizes empathy and understanding. His book, *Nonviolent Communication: A Language of Life,* teaches readers how to resolve conflicts peacefully and build stronger relationships.

Amy Marschall, PsyD – Dr. Amy Marschall is a clinical psychologist who specializes in working with children and adolescents. Her work, featured on the website Verywell Mind, focuses on techniques for de-escalating conflicts by addressing underlying emotions and promoting active listening.

Tatiana Astray, PhD – Dr. Tatiana Astray is known for her research and practical tools for de-escalating conflicts. Her book, *Mastering Conflict Resolution: Strategies for De-escalation,* provides effective techniques for ensuring all parties feel heard and understood.

Mira Kirshenbaum – Mira Kirshenbaum is a psychotherapist and author known for her work on relationships and conflict resolution. Her book, *The Gift of a Year,* offers insights into addressing emotional needs and improving communication in personal and professional settings.

OTHER RESOURCES

For more detailed insights, refer to the resources from *Psychology Today* and the website, Calmerry, which offer valuable guidance on emotional validation and conflict resolution.

https://www.psychologytoday.com/us/blog/building-a-life-worth-living/202401/the-interpersonal-superpower-of-validation

https://calmerry.com/blog/emotions/the-power-of-emotional-validation-why-we-need-it-and-how-to-practice-it/

https://www.psychologytoday.com/us/basics/emotional-validation

Chapter 9:
Practice Nine, Interdependency

THE SPIRITUALLY CENTERED HIGHER-LEVEL PASSIONATE AND INSPIRING LEADER

ELEMENT FOUR: PASSIONATE AND INSPIRING ⟁

IGNITE PASSION AND DRIVE WITHIN OTHERS, INSPIRING CREATIVITY AND MOTIVATION

Growing up as a Gen Xer, I saw a lot of scandals that made me skeptical about trusting others. Events like Watergate in the 70s, the Iran-Contra Affair in the 80s, and public embarrassments involving people like Jimmy Swaggart and Mel Gibson made me hesitant to have role models. By the time I met Walter in 1989, I was pretty jaded.

Even though I found it hard to trust, meeting Walter was a significant marker in my life. I loved him because he showed me what it meant to connect with others, a concept that I learned to appreciate deeply. It's not just about relying on people; it's about building relationships that benefit everyone involved. Let me explain how this works in different areas of life.

In business, teamwork is like a magic formula that makes everything work better. Picture a team where each person has a special skill. When these skills are combined, the group's output is much greater than what each person could do alone. Walter was great at encouraging this in all of us. For example, he recognized the unique strengths that each person had and made sure we were able to use our talents effectively. He encouraged open discussions in meetings, brainstorming different ideas for creative solutions.

In personal relationships, this mutual support is what holds us together. It builds trust and a sense of security. When you know you can count on someone during tough times, your bond is much stronger. This support encourages each person to reach their full potential. Resolving conflicts becomes easier in a relationship built on this principle. Recognizing the importance of interdependency motivates people to work through their differences, making it easier to find common ground.

This idea isn't just limited to personal relationships or business; it extends to society as a whole. Communities thrive on support systems like social services, volunteer groups, and community organizations. These collaboratives bring people together and improve everyone's well-being. Shared values and common goals unite us for the greater good, making society stronger and more resilient.

Someone has to step up and be a role model; for me, Walter was that person. He showed me that building connections is a powerful force. His actions and guidance demonstrated how encouraging teamwork and trust leads to incredible achievements. Walter's example taught me the importance of mutual support and collaboration, inspiring my value system. Do you have a mentor that you can model? Maybe you're a natural influencer who might be the guiding light for someone else.

TEAM TRIUMPH:
HOW EMMA THE PEACE PRO, SARAH THE
CYCLING CAPTAIN, AND JACKSON THE
MINDFUL MAESTRO TRANSFORMED THEIR WORLD

Sarah, the project coordinator, Emma, the project manager, and Jackson, the boss, were getting into a steady rhythm. Each had their own strengths and areas of growth. The self-awareness and mindfulness practices were paying off. Jackson had been much better at taming his temper, although it wasn't always perfect. His appropriate workplace vulnerability and the way he communicated were inspirational for the team, which bonded them closer together. Emma had also made progress in her mindfulness practices, and her team could feel the difference, especially the not-so-new-anymore Sarah.

Over time, Sarah improved significantly in her role. She became more organized and efficient, thanks to Jackson's guidance. She also developed better communication skills and built stronger relationships with her coworkers. The contrast from when Sarah was newly on the job, lacking confidence, to an accountable, proficient, white-collar made her an invaluable part of the team. She took pride in her work and was mentoring a new part-time staffer. Seeing the part-time person struggle with a project, Sarah offered her assistance. She shared tips and organizational strategies she had learned from Jackson, helping the part-time guy break down the project into manageable tasks.

In addition to helping the part-timer, Sarah also supported Jackson when he needed it. He was preparing a big presentation for an upcoming meeting and had a lot on his plate. Sarah stepped in to help gather data, create slides, and even rehearse the presentation with him. Her assistance was irreplicable, and Jackson was able to deliver a memorable presentation.

Jackson's improvements didn't just happen at work. At home, he became a more present dad and partner. His mindfulness practices helped him be in the moment with his family. He spent quality time with his kids, helping with homework and attending their activities. His partner noticed the change, too, appreciating his calmness and attention, which strengthened their relationship.

Emma took her improved skills beyond the workplace as well. She was passionate about community organizing and decided to use her new skills to help with local events. Emma started volunteering at a community center, where she helped plan events and coordinate volunteers. Her ability to remain calm under pressure and de-escalate tense situations with volunteers made a big difference. She developed a reputation around town as Emma the Peace Pro.

Sarah's newfound confidence and skills extended beyond the workplace. Since she was first able to peddle a bike as a child, Sarah had been passionate about cycling and had recently joined a local cycling team. Thanks to her improved organizational skills, Sarah quickly became a leader in the group. Her ability to coordinate rides, communicate, and motivate team members led her to be named captain. Sarah's leadership brought the team closer together, they achieved better results in their races.

One sunny weekend, Sarah organized a charity ride for the team. She used the skills she had learned from Jackson to plan the event meticulously. She coordinated with local businesses for sponsorships, mapped out the route, and communicated the event around town. The charity ride was a huge success, raising a significant amount of money for Emma's local cause.

Back at work, the positive influence of Sarah, Emma, and Jackson continued to grow. The team became more cohesive and productive thanks to the collaborative environment they had created. Sarah helped Emma with another challenging project involving a tight deadline. Jackson continued to thrive as a leader. The team's success was a testament to the power of how *Allied we can* make a huge impact.

Find a group of people who challenge
and inspire you, spend a lot of time with
them, and it will change your life.

—AMY POEHLER

CHIT-CHAT CHAMPIONS:
MASTERING ACTIVE LISTENING AND OPEN-ENDED QUESTIONS

Ready to boost your communication skills? This guide will help you become a pro at active listening and asking open-ended questions. These skills will make your conversations more meaningful and enjoyable. You'll learn to really hear what others are saying and ask questions that get them talking. By following this guide, you'll feel more confident in your interactions, understand others better, and create connections that matter. Let's get started and watch your communication skills soar!

Most people do not listen with the intent to understand; they listen with the intent to reply.

—STEPHEN R. COVEY

GUIDE TO IMPROVING INTERPERSONAL COMMUNICATIONS
ACTIVE LISTENING AND ASKING OPEN-ENDED QUESTIONS

Overall Goal: *Enhance interpersonal communication skills by developing active listening abilities and the art of asking open-ended questions.*

Part 1: Active Listening – Getting Started

Goal: *Improve your ability to listen actively to others, ensuring you fully understand and engage with their message.*

Activity:

Practice active listening techniques in a conversation with a colleague or friend.

Reflective Exercise:

After the conversation, reflect on how well you listened. Did you maintain eye contact? Did you avoid interrupting? Did you provide feedback that showed you understood the speaker's message?

Example Application – Sarah:

Sarah is having a conversation with her colleague about a project update. She maintains eye contact, nods, and says, *"I see,"* and *"That makes sense,"* to show she is engaged. When her colleague finishes, Sarah summarizes what she heard to confirm her understanding: *"So, you're saying the deadline has been moved to next Friday, and we need to prioritize the client's feedback before then, right?"*

Part 2: Asking Open-Ended Questions – Getting Started

Goal: *Enhance the depth and quality of conversations by asking questions that encourage detailed and thoughtful responses.*

Activity:

Prepare and use open-ended questions in your next conversation with a team member or friend. Focus on questions that start with *"how," "what," "why," or "describe."*

Reflective Exercise:

After the conversation, reflect on the questions you asked. Did they prompt detailed responses? How did the open-ended questions affect the flow of the conversation?

Example Application – Jackson:

Jackson is discussing a new project with his manager. Instead of asking, *"Did you like the proposal?"* he asks, *"What aspects of the proposal do you think will be most beneficial for our client?"* This encourages his manager to provide a detailed response, leading to a richer discussion about the proposal's strengths.

Seek first to understand, then to be understood.

—STEPHEN R. COVEY

Part 1: Active Listening – Going Further

Goal: *Further refine active listening skills by focusing on nonverbal cues and emotional understanding.*

Activity:

Engage in a conversation that involves focusing not only on the words being spoken but also on the speaker's body language and emotional tone.

Reflective Exercise:

Reflect on how well you interpreted the speaker's nonverbal cues. Did you notice any signs of discomfort or enthusiasm? How did you respond to these cues?

Example Application – Emma:

Emma is talking to her friend about a personal issue. She notices her friend's slumped shoulders and quiet tone, indicating sadness. Emma leans in slightly, maintains a soft and supportive tone, and says, *"It sounds like you've been feeling really down lately. Do you want to talk more about what's been going on?"*

Part 2: Asking Open-Ended Questions – Going Further

Goal: *Develop the ability to ask follow-up open-ended questions that build on the speaker's responses.*

Activity:

In your next conversation, practice asking follow-up questions based on the speaker's answers to keep the conversation flowing and gain deeper insights.

Reflective Exercise:

Reflect on the effectiveness of your follow-up questions. Did they help to uncover more details? How did the speaker respond to your follow-up questions?

Example Application – Sarah:

Sarah is having a meeting with her team about a new project strategy. After asking, *"What are your initial thoughts on this approach?"* she follows up with, *"Can you describe any specific challenges you foresee with this strategy?"* This helps to identify potential issues early on and encourages team members to think critically about the plan.

Improving interpersonal communication through active listening and asking open-ended questions significantly enhances your interactions. You'll develop more meaningful and productive conversations, engage in practical activities, reflect on your experiences, and apply these skills in real-life scenarios.

HOW EMPATHETIC ARE YOU REALLY? FIND OUT NOW!

Think you're nailing empathy in every interaction? It's easy to assume, but are you truly connecting with others? Take our Empathy Quiz and discover if you're an empathy ace or if there's still some room to fine-tune your skills. Get your score, along with personalized insights to strengthen those emotional connections. It's like a check-up for your empathy levels—no judgment, just growth! Your friends, family, and colleagues will thank you, and who knows, you might just unlock a whole new level of understanding. Ready to find out?

bit.ly/getyourempathyscore

Listening is an art that requires attention
over talent, spirit over ego, others over self.

—DEAN JACKSON

THE INTERDEPENDENCE PLAYBOOK: FUN AND EFFECTIVE EXERCISES FOR TEAM SYNERGY

The Interdependence Playbook—your guide to building a cohesive, collaborative, and high-performing team. This guide is designed for managers, executives, and leaders who want to enhance their group's interdependence through engaging and insightful exercises. By participating in these activities, you'll foster better communication, stronger relationships, and a deeper understanding of each team member's role.

Improve problem-solving, increase empathy, and take a more unified approach to achieving goals. Imagine an environment where everyone feels valued and works seamlessly toward common objectives—that's the power of interdependence.

FUN IN BUILDING INTERDEPENDENCE

Enhance teamwork and understanding among managers, executives, and leaders to foster collaboration and interdependence.

1. Knowledge Sharing

Goal: *Improve awareness of team members' projects and contributions.*

Activity: Team Memory Game

Instructions:

- Each team member shares an interesting fact about a recent project they worked on.

- After everyone has shared, take turns trying to recall each person's fact.

Reflective Exercise:

- Write down one new thing you learned about each team member's work.

- Discuss how knowing these details helps you collaborate better, such as through better communication, conflict resolution, building on trust, motivating and inspiring each other, and empowering each other.

Benefits:

- **Enhanced Communication:** This exercise helps improve communication by encouraging team members to listen actively and remember details about each other's work.

- **Increased Empathy:** Understanding what others are working on fosters empathy and appreciation for the efforts of different team members.

- **Building Relationships:** Sharing personal achievements and learning about others helps build stronger interpersonal relationships within the team.

Example Application:

During a strategic planning meeting, knowing each department's recent achievements helps in aligning goals and resources effectively.

2. Understanding Roles

Goal: *Gain a deeper understanding of different roles within the team.*

Activity: Role Reversal Discussion

Instructions:

- Pair up with another leader and explain your role in a major project.

- Then, switch and explain each other's roles to the rest of the team.

Reflective Exercise:

- Make notes about what you learned about your partner's role.

- Discuss how understanding different roles improves teamwork and project outcomes.

Benefits:

- **Role Clarity:** By understanding the responsibilities and challenges of different roles, team members better appreciate the contributions of their colleagues.

- **Enhanced Collaboration:** Knowing the specific functions and needs of each role leads to more effective collaboration and resource allocation.

- **Reduced Conflict:** Misunderstandings and conflicts will be reduced when team members have a clear understanding of each other's roles and responsibilities.

Example Application:

In a cross-functional team, understanding the responsibilities of each role can streamline processes and improve efficiency.

3. Applying Skills

Goal: *Utilize individual skills to solve a common challenge collaboratively.*

Activity: Collaborative Innovation Workshop

Instructions:

- Conduct a workshop where team members brainstorm solutions to a common business challenge.

- Ensure that each member uses their unique skills to contribute to the solution.

Reflective Exercise:

- Reflect on how each person's contribution enhanced the final solution.

- Discuss what would happen if any expertise was missing.

Benefits:

- **Leveraging Diverse Skills:** This exercise allows the team to tap into a wide range of skills and perspectives, leading to more innovative solutions.

- **Boosted Creativity:** Collaborative workshops spark creativity by combining different ideas and approaches.

- **Improved Problem-Solving:** Teams solve complex problems more effectively by leveraging the collective expertise of all members.

Example Application:

Combining skills from marketing, design, and engineering in a product development meeting can lead to innovative product features.

4. Analyzing Strategies

Goal: *Develop and analyze different strategies for solving complex business challenges.*

Activity: Problem-Solving Circle

Instructions:

- Present a complex business challenge (e.g., entering a new market).
- Break into small groups to develop solutions, then come back together to analyze each group's approach.

Reflective Exercise:

- Make notes about the different strategies used by each group.
- Discuss why certain strategies were more effective and how they can be implemented.

Benefits:

- **Enhanced Critical Thinking:** Analyzing different strategies helps team members develop critical thinking skills.
- **Better Decision-Making:** By evaluating various approaches, teams make more informed and effective decisions.
- **Learning from Peers:** Team members learn from each other's strategies and experiences, improving their own problem-solving abilities.

Example Application:

Analyzing different market entry strategies helps identify the most viable approach for expanding business operations.

5. Evaluating Perspectives

Goal: *Evaluate different viewpoints to make better strategic decisions.*

Activity: Team Debate

Instructions:

- Split into two teams and debate a topic related to business strategy (e.g., the benefits of remote work vs. in-office work).

- Each team presents their arguments and then evaluates the other team's points.

Reflective Exercise:

- Reflect on the strengths and weaknesses of both arguments.

- Make notes about how evaluating different viewpoints leads to better strategic decisions.

Benefits:

- **Diverse Perspectives:** Debating different viewpoints helps expose team members to a variety of perspectives and ideas.

- **Improved Persuasion Skills:** Team members practice articulating and defending their ideas, enhancing their persuasive abilities.

- **Balanced Decisions:** Evaluating multiple perspectives leads to more balanced and well-rounded decision-making.

Example Application:

Debating different approaches to work arrangements helps in crafting policies that balance productivity and employee satisfaction.

6. Creating Solutions

Goal: Foster creativity and teamwork by developing collaborative solutions.

Activity: Invent a Team Game

Instructions:

- As a team, create a new game that requires collaboration to succeed.
- Write down the rules and play the game together.

Reflective Exercise:

- Reflect on how the game required teamwork and the strategies used.
- Discuss what worked well and what could be improved.

Benefits:

- **Encourages Creativity:** Designing a game together encourages creative thinking and problem-solving.
- **Strengthens Team Bonds**: Playing and creating games helps build stronger relationships and improve team cohesion.
- **Demonstrates Collaboration:** The exercise highlights the importance of working together and leveraging each other's strengths.

Example Application:

In a leadership retreat, creating and playing a collaborative game highlights the importance of teamwork and strategic thinking in a fun setting.

Life doesn't make any sense without interdependence. We need each other, and the sooner we learn that the better for us all.

—ERIK H. ERIKSON

ANT-TASTIC INTERDEPENDENCE:
HOW WE CAN OVERCOME FEAR AND THRIVE TOGETHER!

Imagine a world without ants. Without their presence, many ecosystems would crumble. Ants work together in highly organized colonies, performing various tasks that keep their environment balanced. They aerate the soil, which helps plants grow by allowing air and water to reach the roots. Ants also help with seed dispersal, which promotes plant diversity and growth. Without ants, soil quality declines, plant growth slows, and animals relying on those plants struggle. As this cascading effect continues, it disrupts entire ecosystems.

Now, let's switch gears to human society. In the U.S., we pride ourselves on doing things independently, it's been ingrained in us since our forefathers staked their claim on North America. For generations, we've been taught to be self-made. Messages like *"pull yourself up by the bootstraps"* and *"If it's to be, it's up to me"* have seeped into our subconscious. We even have a holiday commemorating "Independence Day." While being independent has its strengths, taken to extremes, it has dismal consequences.

Humans, like ants, need each other. Picture a family where everyone pitches in—parents take care of the children, and everyone helps with the chores. Or think about a sports team where each player has a unique role, scores goals, and wins games together. Perhaps a group of engineers designing a building that's taller than the Burj Khalifa in Dubai, each contributes their creativity. But let's be real— sometimes, being interdependent is tough. We might feel like being vulnerable and asking for help is a sign of weakness.

People often struggle to be open in social settings because they fear judgment and rejection. For example, in a school group project, students don't share their ideas because they worry about being laughed at. This lack of communication leads to misunderstandings and conflicts, making it hard for the group to work together.

At work, a boss who doesn't consider their employees' feelings or personal struggles has a tough time giving an employee a break when a family member needs care. This lack of empathy and compassion creates a toxic environment.

Our inability to forgive also hinders interdependence. Picture two coworkers who have a disagreement. One holds a grudge, creating ongoing tension that affects the whole team.

Another obstacle is not being genuine. If a person pretends to be someone they're not to fit in, it creates suspicion and distrust. Authenticity builds trust, and without it, relationships can't thrive. For example, someone who claims to be competent in a critical task fails at it and doesn't take ownership, embarrassing the whole group.

In the end, it all boils down to fear—fear of judgment, rejection, vulnerability, and failure. Overcoming fear requires self-awareness[2], courage, and the willingness to embrace vulnerability.[3]

We begin these new pathways by reflecting on and acknowledging our fears without judgment.[4] We start to share our thoughts and feelings with trusted friends, testing the waters of vulnerability in a safe environment. This practice gradually builds our confidence, showing us that being open and honest leads to deeper connections.

In the workplace, empathy and compassion become guiding principles.[5] A boss who once struggled to understand their employees' personal hurdles now makes a conscious effort to listen

---

[2] Chapter 1

[3] Chapter 3

[4] Chapter 2

[5] Chapter 4

and support them. Similarly, when individuals take responsibility for their mistakes, they build trust and reliability within their teams.[6]

As we continue to grow, we learn the importance of forgiveness.[7] Holding onto past grievances only creates barriers to healthy relationships. We make room for positive interactions and collaboration by letting go of grudges. Authenticity becomes a cornerstone of our interactions, allowing us to be true to ourselves.[8]

Ultimately, overcoming fear is about facing it head-on and choosing to act despite it. It's about realizing that, just as ants thrive through their interdependence, humans achieve incredible things when we work together. We create a connected, compassionate, and successful world by finding common ground, supporting each other, and celebrating our interdependence.

---

[6] Chapter 7

[7] Chapter 5

[8] Chapter 6

Alone we can do so little, together, we can do so much.

—HELEN KELLER

RESOURCES

AUTHORS AND EXPERTS ON INTERDEPENDENCE

Understanding how everything and everyone is connected really changes the way we see the world. By exploring the ideas of interdependence and interconnectedness, we learn how our actions impact others and how we build stronger communities. These concepts show us that nothing exists in isolation; instead, everything is part of a larger web of relationships. When we start to see these connections, we make better decisions that benefit us and those around us.

If you're finding navigating this web of interdependence challenging and want to enhance your ability to work effectively with others, seeking coaching help is incredibly beneficial. A coach provides you with personalized strategies to improve your communication, build stronger relationships, and create a positive impact in your community.

Drawing inspiration from various experts and authors, such as those listed below, deepen your understanding of these themes. They offer valuable insights that are crucial for building interdependent relationships. By embracing the teachings of these thought leaders, you will transform your approach to interdependence and make a meaningful impact.

The Things They Carried **by Tim O'Brien** – Tim O'Brien is a Vietnam War veteran and writer. His book *The Things They Carried* shares stories about soldiers in the Vietnam War, highlighting the strong bonds and connections they form in tough times.

Indra's Net **by Rajiv Malhotra** – Rajiv Malhotra is a researcher and writer. In *Indra's Net*, he explores the idea of interconnectedness in Indian philosophy, explaining how everything in the universe is linked together like a giant web.

Connected: The Surprising Power of Our Social Networks and How They Shape Our Lives **by Nicholas A. Christakis and James H. Fowler** – Nicholas Christakis and James Fowler are sociologists. Their book *Connected* shows how social networks influence our lives and highlights the power of our connections with others.

Interconnected: Embracing Life in Our Global Society **by Ogyen Trinley Dorje** – **Ogyen Trinley Dorje**, the 17th Karmapa of Tibetan Buddhism, writes about the importance of interconnectedness today. His book *Interconnected* combines Buddhist wisdom with modern issues, encouraging a compassionate and connected world.

Emergent Strategy **by Adrienne Maree Brown** – Adrienne Maree Brown is a writer and activist. In *Emergent Strategy,* she discusses how interconnectedness and teamwork can help create positive social change, drawing ideas from nature and systems theory.

The Relationship Cure **by John Gottman** – This book provides a five-step program for improving relationships with spouses, family members, friends, and even colleagues. It introduces the concept of "emotional bids" and emphasizes the importance of recognizing and responding to these bids to enhance emotional connections.

The Hidden Life of Trees **by Peter Wohlleben** – Peter Wohlleben is a German forester and writer. His book *The Hidden Life of Trees* reveals how trees communicate and help each other, showing the amazing ways in which nature is interconnected.

Global Interdependence **by Akira Iriye** – Akira Iriye is a historian who looks at how the world became interconnected after World War II. In

Global Interdependence, he explains how people, cultures, and nations are linked together, shaping the modern world in surprising ways.

Reading about interdependence and interconnectedness helps us appreciate the power of relationships and teamwork. Whether it's in nature, society, or our personal lives, recognizing how things are linked can lead to more joy and success. By applying these lessons, we can create a world where everyone thrives, understanding that our well-being is tied to the well-being of others. These insights remind us that by working together and valuing our connections, we can achieve great things and make a positive impact on the world.

Chapter 10:
Practice Ten, Re-Purpose

THE SPIRITUALLY CENTERED HIGHER-LEVEL PASSIONATE AND INSPIRING LEADER

ELEMENT FOUR: PASSIONATE AND INSPIRING ⬙

IGNITE PASSION AND DRIVE WITHIN OTHERS, INSPIRING CREATIVITY AND MOTIVATION

For me, one of the most interesting parts of life is how our sense of purpose changes over time. As I've moved through my 20s, 30s, 40s, and now into my 50s, I've learned that purpose isn't something that stays the same. It changes as our lives change, as we go through different experiences, and hopefully grow wiser from them.

When we're younger, we often see purpose in a simple way. It's shaped by the dreams we have as kids and the goals we set as teenagers. I remember when people used to ask, *"What do you want to be when you grow up?"* My answer was simple back then—I wanted to swoop in like a superhero and save the day. These dreams were fueled by a sense of invincibility, the belief that anything was possible. Back then, My sense of purpose was having fun, seeking excitement, and adventure.

As I transitioned into my teenage years, my understanding of purpose began to shift. It was no longer just about fantastical heroics but about discovering who I was and what truly interested me. My purpose became intertwined with exploring my passions and learning more about the world around me. This was a time of experimentation and self-discovery, where purpose took on a deeper meaning.

Then came the military, a pivotal point in my life where purpose became service to our country. I was also driven by leaving home and making my mark as an independent young man. The camaraderie, discipline, and sense of duty I developed during that time shaped my understanding of purpose in profound new ways.

As I transitioned from full-time military service to the active Army Reserve in my 20s, I found myself caught up in a fun-driven lifestyle, making decisions that were at odds with the values I hadn't yet redefined. These short-term choices came at the high price of my long-term dreams.

During this period, I found a job at a music distribution company, where I met Walter. He taught me that being an effective leader wasn't just about achieving goals but also about making meaningful connections.

After leaving the music industry in my 30s, I found moderate success in different sales jobs. Eventually, I took a position at a business non-profit, where I felt good about contributing to something bigger than myself. Those were some very rewarding, purpose-driven years.

Later, I moved to the Southwest and took a job in the financial services industry. I experienced a big bump in pay, but it also marked the most miserable period of my work life. My focus shifted from meaningful work to mostly monetary rewards, and it was during that time that my alcohol and substance use escalated. My career and personal life became a reflection of conflicting values in action. While my job wasn't fulfilling, I found a sense of purpose in contributing to the cycling team that I was a member of. However, even with this outlet, I still struggled. I longed for the meaningful life that I had previously experienced.

I admitted to myself that I needed help. I couldn't figure out how to break free from discontentment and frustration. I sought counseling, self-help programs, and personal coaching, all of which marked a time of real growth for me. This inner work helped me to re-purpose once again.

One of the hardest things about trying to live a purpose-driven life is dealing with conflicting desires. When our values don't line up, it's difficult to make decisions that align with what we really want. This kind of conflict pulls us in different directions, and we sprint away from fulfillment. For example, if career success and family time are at odds, we can end up sacrificing one for the other, leading to guilt and frustration. It's hard to be in and enjoy the moment with this inner conflict.

Now, in the second half of my life, I'm re-purposing once again. It's not just about *"What do I want to achieve?"* but also *"What legacy do I want to leave behind?"* I'm compelled to mentor the next generation, sharing what I've learned and helping others find their way. Spirituality has also become really important to me, and it's guiding me to help others on their spiritual pathways.

One thing remains constant throughout these life stages—the need to redefine my purpose during significant milestones. This requires self-awareness, mindfulness, and a willingness to be vulnerable. It's about asking the tough questions—"What problem do I want to solve?"—and being open to the answers, even if they lead me down the path of uncertainty.

Realizing how my actions affect others taught me that purpose isn't just about personal success; it's about contributing to the greater good. In the end, living a fulfilling life, is continually growing, making the necessary changes, and tuning into what matters the most.

The two most important days in your life are the day you are born and the day you find out why.

—MARK TWAIN

SWINGING AT LIFE'S CURVEBALLS: RECALIBRATING YOUR AIM TO AVOID PURPOSE PITFALLS

So, let's say that we're doing what we think is a good job of being current with our values and moving in the right direction with purpose. But what happens when life throws us a curveball? Whether we're ready or not, when the unexpected arrives, our sense of purpose is challenged and reshaped in ways we never anticipated. Life cycles and events—like the loss of a loved one, a career setback, or a personal crisis—can drastically alter our trajectory. Often painful and unwelcome, these moments force us to re-evaluate what truly matters. They demand digging deep and questioning whether the pathway we've been on still aligns with our evolving values and the new uncertain reality we face.

Take, for example, someone who has spent years climbing the corporate ladder, and focused on career success and financial goals. Suddenly, an unexpected health scare or the responsibility of caring for an aging parent turns that purpose upside down. The things that once seemed so important—promotions, awards, and making money—start to lose their meaning in light of new priorities. The challenge isn't just recognizing the shift but accepting it and letting a new purpose emerge. It's about letting go of what no longer helps us and embracing the uncertainty of a new direction. Not easy!

Similarly, life transitions like becoming a parent or entering retirement spark a profound re-purposing of our lives. A new parent might find that their purpose shifts from personal achievement to nurturing and guiding their child. Suddenly, values shift, they have more patience, empathy, and selflessness becoming central rather than ambition or independence. Though filled with joy, these transitions also bring a sense of loss for the person we used to be or the goals we used to have.

Societal and global events also force us to re-examine our purpose. The recent global pandemic led many to question their previous paths and reconsider what they truly value. For some, the purpose shifted from career-driven ambitions to prioritizing health, family, and community. For others, it sparked a desire to make a bigger impact, leading to changes in their career, lifestyle, or even where they live.

Living through these challenges and unforeseen events teaches us that purpose isn't a static destination but a fluid journey. Recognizing that while we may not have control over the events that shape our lives, we do have control over how we respond to them. By staying true to our core values, even as they evolve, we navigate these changes and emerge with a renewed sense of purpose that reflects who we truly are.

Living life on autopilot without considering whether our values are aligned is very risky. When we go through life without clear conscious intention, it's easy for outside events or other people to decide our purpose for us. We might find ourselves chasing goals that aren't really ours just because it's what society, bosses, family, or circumstances expect of us. Over time, this leads to a life that feels out of sync with who we really are, creating feelings of emptiness, disconnection, or even resentment. That's why it's so important to regularly check in with ourselves, making sure our actions and choices match our core values and that we're living a life true to our authentic selves.

bit.ly/newyoucourse

So, if you find yourself feeling lost or conflicted, it's a sign that it's time to re-purpose. It's an invitation to reassess your values, realign your life with them, and embrace the new direction that life is nudging you toward. By doing so, you transform obstacles into opportunities for growth and create a life that is not only purpose-driven but also deeply fulfilling.

Your life is your story. Write well. Edit often.

—SUSAN STATHAM

THE METAMORPHOSIS OF HIGHER-LEVEL LEADERSHIP: HOW PURPOSE EVOLVES

Key Takeaways:

- **Purpose evolves:** It changes as we go through different stages of life.

- **Self-awareness[9]:** Mindfulness[10], compassion[11], and forgiveness[12] help redefine our purpose.

- **Interdependency[13]:** Building connections enhances our sense of purpose.

- By finding our purpose and aligning our actions with it, we can lead meaningful lives and inspire others to do the same.

PURPOSE PURSUIT: EMBRACING LIFE'S TWISTS

Finding your purpose starts with self-awareness and mindfulness. It's all about answering the big question, *"What problem do I want to solve?"* Remember, your purpose isn't static—it changes as you move through different stages of life.

Perhaps when you were a kid, someone asked, *"What do you want to do when you grow up?"* You responded then, but your answer changed as you changed. You quickly learned that purpose evolves when life presents new challenges.

---

[9] More in Chapter One

[10] More in Chapter Two

[11] More in Chapter Four

[12] More in Chapter Five

[13] More in Chapter Nine

- **As a child,** it might mean imagining yourself as a superhero saving the day.

- **As a teenager,** it could mean figuring out your interests and passions.

- **As a young adult,** it becomes about choosing a career path.

- **As a career-focused person,** it's about advancing and making an impact in your chosen field.

- **As a life partner,** it involves building a life together and supporting each other's dreams.

- **As a parent,** it means guiding and nurturing your children.

- **As someone entering the second half of life,** it's about reflecting on your journey and finding deeper meaning in your experiences.

Here's a list of the character traits and attributes that I've found best describe purpose-driven people:

Passion: Enthusiasm and Energy

Think of passion as the fuel in your tank. When you're passionate about something, you're riding a wave of energy that keeps you going, no matter how tough things get. Having an endless supply of enthusiasm propels you forward, making you unstoppable.

Resilience: Persistence and Grit

Resilience is a superpower that helps you bounce back from setbacks. Picture yourself as a rubber band—no matter how much you're stretched or pulled, you snap back into shape. This grit ensures you don't lose sight of your goals, even when the going gets tough.

Authenticity: Integrity and Honesty [14]

Being authentic means staying true to who you are. It's the compass that points north, guiding you through life's decisions. When you act with integrity, people trust you and believe in you because they know you're honest and genuine.

Visionary: Forward Thinking

Having a vision is the map for your journey. You know where you want to go, and you can see the big picture. This clarity helps you make decisions that align with your long-term goals, ensuring every step you take is in the right direction.

Empathy: Walking in Someone Else's Shoes

Empathy is the ability to imagine yourself in someone else's shoes. Imagine having a magic mirror that lets you see the world through others' eyes. This ability helps you connect deeply with people, making you a supportive and understanding friend or leader.

---

[14] More in Chapter Six

Self-Discipline: Focus and Control

Self-discipline is your secret weapon for staying focused. It's having blinders that keep you from getting distracted by all the noise around you. This control helps you prioritize what's important, making sure you stay on track toward your goals.

Curiosity: Open-mindedness and Learning

Curiosity is the spark that keeps you exploring and learning new things. Think of it as having a pair of binoculars that let you see the world in a new light. You are always searching for new ideas and experiences. This open-mindedness fuels your growth and innovation.

Adaptability: Flexibility and Versatility

Adaptability allows you to adjust to any situation. Life throws curveballs, but with flexibility, you can pivot and change your plans as needed. It's a crucial skill for navigating the ever-changing landscape of life.

Altruism: Generosity and Selflessness

Altruism is about putting others before yourself. It's having a big heart that overflows with kindness and generosity. When you act selflessly, you create a ripple effect of positive change, making the world a better place for everyone.

DISCOVERING YOUR "WHY": A FUN GUIDE TO UNLEASHING YOUR PURPOSE

Have you ever felt like you're moving through life on autopilot, not really sure why you're doing what you're doing? Finding your purpose brings clarity to your life. This guide will help you uncover the deeper reasons behind your actions, making every day more meaningful. By following these steps, you'll gain insights into what truly drives you and how to align your life with your passions and values.

Are you ready to reap the benefits of contributing to something greater than yourself? Let's start to uncover your unique "why"!

1. Remembering: Self-Reflection

- **Identify Your Values and Passions:** Think about what truly matters to you. What activities or causes make you feel most alive? Write down these important aspects of your life.

    - ○ *Exercise:* **Value Discovery:** List your top ten values. Then, narrow them down to your top three. Reflect on why these are most important to you. The **New Values in Motion assessmen**t is available to help you get crystal clear about your values so you can learn how to live in alignment with what really matters to you.

bit.ly/NMPvalues

- **Journaling:** Keep a journal to write down your thoughts and experiences regularly. Over time, you'll start seeing patterns that reveal your deeper interests and values.

    - ○ *Exercise:* **Daily Reflection:** Spend 10 minutes each night writing about what made you happy or proud that day. Over the next few weeks, look for recurring themes.

2. Understanding: Set Goals Based on Your Values

- **Long-Term Planning:** Think about your future and set goals that reflect your values. Whether you're seeking career growth, personal development, or helping your community, make sure your goals align with what truly matters to you.

    - *Exercise:* **Vision Board:** Create a vision board with images and words that represent your goals and dreams. Place it somewhere you'll see it every day.

- **Small, Actionable Steps:** Break down your big goals into smaller, manageable tasks. This will make the journey less overwhelming, and each step forward will feel like a victory.

    - *Exercise:* **Weekly Action Plan:** Write down three small actions you'll take toward your larger goals each week. Celebrate each completed step! Scan the QR code to our Values in Motion Planner.

        bit.ly/valuesactionplan

Example: Create a vision board focused on finding a charity that supports underserved communities and aligns with your values of compassion and social impact, including images of outreach and testimonials. Begin by researching local charities that match your values and setting up informational calls to learn more about their missions. Each day, spend 10 minutes researching charities and journaling your thoughts. Each week, reach out to at least one charity and schedule a visit or volunteer opportunity.

3. Applying: Seek Inspirations

- **Read Biographies:** Learn about people who have lived purpose-driven lives. Their stories can inspire you and offer practical lessons to apply in your own life.

  - ○ **Exercise: Biography Review:** Read a biography of someone you admire. Write a short summary or list of what inspired you most about their journey.

- **Talk to Inspiring People:** Engage with mentors or role models. Their wisdom will guide you through your journey.

  - ○ *Exercise:* **Informational Interviews:** Schedule conversations with people you look up to. Ask them about their path and any advice they have for finding purpose.

Side note: Most people love to talk about themselves, and it will make them feel connected to you. Think ahead about a few questions to ask, for example: How did you get here? What path brought you here?

4. Analyzing: Engage in Experiences

- **Volunteering:** Giving your time to causes you care about will help you discover where your passions lie and how helping others brings joy and meaning to your life.

  - ○ *Exercise*: **Volunteer Match:** Choose a cause you care about and commit to volunteering regularly. Reflect on how it makes you feel and what you learned from it.

- **Try New Things:** Experiment with new activities and adventures. Exploration is key to uncovering hidden interests and potential purposes.

  - ○ *Exercise:* **Hobby Exploration:** Pick a new hobby or activity each month. Keep a journal of what you enjoyed about it and what you learned from each experience.

5. Evaluating: Mindfulness and Meditation

- **Mindfulness Practices:** Staying connected to your present experiences helps to understand what truly brings you fulfillment.

  - o *Exercise:* **Daily Mindfulness:** Spend a few minutes each day practicing mindfulness. Focus on your breath and observe your thoughts without judgment.

- **Meditation**: Regular meditation helps to clear your mind, allowing you to see your path more clearly and understand deeper motivations.

  - o *Exercise:* **Guided Meditation:** Use guided meditation apps or videos to help you focus and reflect on your purpose and goals.

6. Creating: Feedback and Reflection

- **Seek Feedback:** Talk to friends, family, or colleagues about your journey. They might see strengths and interests in you that you haven't noticed.

  ○ **Feedback Session:** Schedule a meeting with trusted friends or mentors to discuss your progress and gather their insights.

- **Reflect on Feedback:** Consider how this external input aligns with your inner thoughts. Use this reflection to adjust your course to your true purpose.

  ○ *Exercise:* **Reflection Journal:** After receiving feedback, write down your thoughts and feelings. Reflect on how you will incorporate this feedback into your journey.

So ...what fires you up? What keeps you going strong? Finding your purpose is a never-ending adventure, and it kicks off with knowing your "Why." Enjoy the process of discovering and redefining your purpose as you grow and change. The best path is the one that helps you find a meaningful life.

Your purpose in life is not just to exist, but
to thrive and to do so with some passion, some
compassion, some humor, and some style.

—MAYA ANGELOU

TYING IT ALL TOGETHER WITH PURPOSE AND POISE

In the ever-evolving city of Dallas, there was a man who had a unique ability to make things better. He wasn't someone who sought the spotlight but rather someone who quietly and purposefully went about his work, driven by a deep sense of mission. His actions weren't about seeking glory or recognition but about creating lasting, meaningful change—something much more impactful.

This man, known for his infectious enthusiasm and unwavering commitment to education, had built a reputation in ways that few could have predicted. He wasn't always front and center, but those who knew him recognized his remarkable talent for seeing potential where others only saw problems. He had a gift for taking on the seemingly impossible and transforming it into something extraordinary. His story is one of persistence, vision, and a deep belief in the power of aligning one's life with core values.

His journey began in Chicago, where he grew up in a household steeped in values. His father and mother taught him the importance of service, integrity, and hard work. These lessons stayed with him as a guiding light through his education and early career. After earning degrees from some of the nation's top institutions, he found himself working in various prestigious roles, including a position in the executive office of a president of the United States. But despite his success, he re-purposed toward something more meaningful that would allow him to use his skills and experiences to truly make a difference.

That pull eventually led him to a small, struggling college that had lost its way and was on the brink of closure. Many would have seen this as a dead-end, but not him. He saw it as an opportunity to bring his values to life and help others.

When he took over as the leader of this college, the challenges were immense. The financial situation was dire, enrollment was plummeting, and morale was at an all-time low. But he saw potential where others saw failure. He believed that education was not just about degrees but about building character and preparing students to make a difference in the world. With this belief, he began to implement changes that eventually transformed the school and, in turn, the lives of the students and community around it.

One of his most innovative ideas was converting the campus's unused football field into a farm. The farm provided fresh produce to the surrounding community, which suffered from a lack of access to healthy food, while teaching students valuable lessons in agriculture, entrepreneurship, and social responsibility. But more than that, it served as a symbol of repurposing lives—of taking something that had been discarded and giving it new meaning. This was his vision: to help people find new pathways.

As the college began to thrive under his leadership, his influence started to extend beyond the campus. His work was recognized on a national level, and soon, his name was mentioned alongside some of the most influential leaders in the world. People began to see him as a visionary, a leader who understood that real change comes from aligning work with values and helping others discover their purpose.

Despite the accolades and recognition, he remained focused on his mission. He knew that his work was far from over, and he continued to push forward, consistently looking for new ways to make an impact. It wasn't about fame or titles for him; it was about making a difference in the lives of others.

The Higher-level Leader Revealed

Dr. Michael Sorrell was the man who transformed that struggling college in Dallas into a thriving institution of purpose-driven education. He was also named one of the world's greatest leaders by *Fortune Magazine*.

Dr. Sorrell's journey to becoming a higher-education leader is deeply rooted in the values his parents instilled in him while growing up in Chicago. His father, a social worker, and his mother, a restaurant owner, taught him the importance of hard work, service, and integrity. These values became the foundation for his future endeavors and shaped his approach to leadership.

Sorrell's educational journey took him from St. Ignatius College Prep in Chicago to Oberlin College, where he earned his bachelor's degree. He then pursued advanced degrees at Duke University, earning both a law degree and a master's in public policy, followed by a doctorate in education from the University of Pennsylvania. His diverse academic background and practical experience, including a role as a special assistant in the Clinton administration, gave him a broad perspective on leadership. However, it was his commitment to values that ultimately defined his career.

In 2007, Sorrell faced the challenge of reviving Paul Quinn College, a historically Black college in Dallas, Texas, which was on the brink of closure. Under his leadership, the college underwent a remarkable transformation. One of his boldest initiatives was the creation of the "WE Over Me Farm," which addressed local food deserts while providing students with valuable skills. His leadership, focused on purpose and values, has revitalized Paul Quinn College and set a new standard for higher education, earning him recognition as one of the world's greatest leaders in 2018.

Solving Today's Puzzles

The world needs more purpose-driven people like Dr. Sorrell to make positive change happen. Imagine if everyone, in their own way, found and thrived on their purpose. A doctor, driven by a passion for healing, could bring both physical relief and emotional comfort to their patients. In a hospital, this could mean patients feel cared for on a deeper level, leading to better recovery outcomes and a more compassionate healthcare environment. An artist with a clear sense of purpose could create works that inspire and uplift entire communities. Art can become a powerful tool for social change, raising awareness and bringing people together.

In every walk of life, from business leaders to community volunteers, from parents to politicians, defining and tuning into our purpose transforms how we live and work. Purpose-driven people inspire others to find their own purpose.

But here's the thing: even with the best intentions, many of us feel like something is holding us back. Do you feel like no matter how hard you try, you can't quite reach your full potential? Limiting beliefs often creep in, creating doubt, fear, and self-sabotage. These thoughts can keep you from thriving in your purpose. But it doesn't have to stay this way.

The **Empowered Beliefs in Motion** mini-course offers a practical, step-by-step system to help you transform those limiting thoughts into empowering ones. In just 5 lessons, you'll build confidence, align your values, and create lasting change. Imagine what it would be like to finally break through those mental barriers and live fully in your purpose.

bit.ly/beliefsinmotion

So, what puzzle do you want to solve? Finding your purpose starts with self-awareness and mindfulness. It's a continuous process, evolving as you move through different stages of life. From imagining yourself as a superhero as a child to finding deeper meaning in your experiences as you grow older, your purpose changes and grows with you.

What talents do you possess that, if shared, would make the world a better place?

Fight for the things that you care about but
do it in a way that will lead others to join you.

—RUTH BADER GINSBURG

RESOURCES

AUTHORS AND EXPERTS ON PURPOSE

Finding your purpose in life can be a transformative experience, opening up new paths and possibilities. Whether you're starting to explore your passions or looking to redefine your values and goals, there are many books and resources to guide you. I've curated several experts who offer practical advice and insights on how to find joy in daily activities, listen to your inner voice, and focus on what truly matters. Check out the resources below and the values guide to the right and get inspired to take meaningful steps toward a fulfilling and purpose-driven life.

bit.ly/valuesinmotionguide

The Values Factor **by Dr. John Demartini** offers a straightforward method to discover and prioritize our true values. By answering reflective questions, we can learn what inspires us and align our lives with these insights for greater fulfillment.

Man's Search for Meaning **by Viktor E. Frankl,** a Holocaust survivor, delves into how finding purpose and meaning in life can help us to endure and transcend even the most brutal experiences. His book combines personal anecdotes with his psychological theories, emphasizing that life has meaning under all circumstances.

Ikigai: The Japanese Secret to a Long and Happy Life **by Hector Garcia and Francesc Miralles** – This book explores the Japanese concept of Ikigai, which represents the intersection of one's passion, mission, vocation, and profession. It offers insights into finding joy and purpose in daily life through balance, harmony, and self-discovery.

***The Untethered Soul: The Journey Beyond Yourself* by Michael A. Singer** – Singer's book provides a spiritual guide to freeing oneself from habitual thoughts and emotions that limit our potential. It encourages readers to explore their inner consciousness and embrace a more expansive state of being, thus discovering a deeper purpose.

***The Artist's Way* by Julia Cameron** – Aimed primarily at creatives, this book is full of exercises designed to help anyone rediscover their creativity and, in turn, their life's purpose. Cameron helps readers uncover personal restrictions and unlock their full potential.

***Let Your Life Speak: Listening for the Voice of Vocation* by Parker J. Palmer** – He shares his personal journey toward finding a purposeful life, stressing the importance of listening to one's inner voice rather than imitating others. This book offers profound insights into living a life that is true to oneself.

***The Path Made Clear: Discovering Your Life's Direction and Purpose* by Oprah Winfrey** – In this inspirational book, Oprah shares her own journey alongside insights from other influential figures. It provides a framework for readers to discover their most profound visions and live a life of significance and purpose.

***Life's Amazing Secrets: How to Find Balance and Purpose in Your Life* by Gaur Gopal Das** – Drawing from his experiences as a monk, Das blends spirituality and practicality to offer readers guidance on navigating life's challenges and finding a balanced and purposeful existence.

***Essentialism: The Disciplined Pursuit of Less* by Greg McKeown** – McKeown challenges the notion that more is better, advocating instead for focusing on what truly matters. His book provides practical advice on eliminating distractions and making deliberate choices to live a more meaningful and fulfilling life.

Getting Grit: The Evidence-Based Approach to Cultivating Passion, Perseverance, and Purpose **by Caroline Adams Miller** – Miller explains how cultivating grit—passion and perseverance toward long-term goals—can help individuals overcome obstacles and achieve a purpose-driven life. Her book is filled with practical strategies for building resilience and staying motivated.

Each person's journey to becoming purpose-driven is unique, and what works for one might not work for another. It's important to try various approaches and remain open to changing your direction as you learn more about yourself.

Conclusion

ALLIED WE CAN FIND COMMON GROUND AND THRIVE

THE AIR IS WARM AND INVITING, filled with the scent of blooming flowers and the gentle babble of a nearby stream. I walk down the path, feeling the soft grass under my feet. Faces light up with genuine smiles as people greet me with warmth and kindness. The community thrives on mutual respect and understanding. The landscape is a beautiful blend of lush greenery and crystal-clear waters. Here, life is an effortless dance of connection and joy, where everyone has found their place and is truly at peace.

This place is called Unityville, the beating heart of this vibrant society where humanity's greatest potential is reached.

I head to breakfast, where neighbors gather to share stories and laughter. There's no rush, just a natural rhythm that flows through the city. I sit with a group of friends, savoring fresh fruits and warm pastries as we chat about our plans for the day.

Today, I decide to join a group of artists painting a mural. The streets are alive with color and creativity. I dip my brush into vibrant hues, feeling the joy of transforming a blank wall into a masterpiece. As we paint, we talk about our inspirations and the stories behind our work. The mural begins to take shape, reflecting the collective spirit of our community.

Later, I wander through the bustling markets where farmers bring their fresh harvests. I stop to chat with a farmer who proudly shows me his organic produce. We laugh as he tells me about the challenges of growing tomatoes this season. I buy a basket of vegetables, knowing that tonight's dinner will be a delicious feast shared with family and friends.

One of the most remarkable things about Unityville is that no one ever lacks anything. Everyone has what they need to thrive. If someone needs help, the community rallies around them, ensuring that every person feels supported and valued. Last week my neighbor's roof needed repairs; within hours, a group of us had tools in hand to fix it.

Trust is the foundation of life in Unityville. There are no locks on doors because there's no need for them. Agreements are made with a handshake, and promises are always kept. When differences arise, they're settled through open conversation, with everyone listening and seeking to understand. The community thrives on mutual respect and a shared commitment to the common good. I recall a recent town hall meeting where we discussed new initiatives for sustainable living. Everyone had a voice, and we reached a consensus through respectful dialogue.

Leadership in Unityville is about guiding with wisdom and integrity. The leaders are deeply connected to the people and the practices that bind us together. They inspire with their actions, leading by example. Decisions are made with the well-being of all in mind, and accountability is a given. This transparent and heartfelt approach to leadership ensures that everyone feels heard and understood. I feel a sense of pride knowing our leaders genuinely care about each one of us.

Community spirit runs deep in Unityville. If someone is going through a tough time, neighbors are there with a comforting word or a helping hand. The bonds between people are strong, and no one ever feels alone. Celebrations are frequent and lively, with music, dancing, and laughter filling the air. Festivals bring everyone together, creating a sense of unity and shared joy. Just last night, we danced under the stars, our hearts full of happiness and connection.

Education in Unityville is seen as an exciting journey that lasts a lifetime. Schools are places of wonder and discovery, where learning is hands-on and engaging. Children and adults alike are encouraged to explore, ask questions, and embrace curiosity. Mistakes are simply part of the learning process, and each day is filled with new opportunities to grow and develop. I spend my afternoons mentoring young students, guiding them in their creative projects, and learning from their fresh perspectives.

As the sun sets over Unityville, the community gathers in the central square. We share our day's experiences, laugh about the funny moments, and dream together about the future. The sky above is a canvas of stars, and the night is filled with the sounds of music and joy. Unityville is a place where life is lived fully and freely, and kindness is the norm.

Constant kindness can accomplish much.
As the sun makes ice melt, kindness causes misunderstanding, mistrust, and hostility to evaporate.

—ALBERT SCHWEITZER

Suddenly, I awaken. The dream fades, and I find myself back in my desert home, the warm glow of the rising sun casting long shadows. The peace and synthesis of Unityville linger in my mind as I sit up and stretch. But as reality sets in, so do my thoughts about the world around me.

I think about the current condition of the United States. It feels like we're on the brink of a dramatic change, not necessarily for the better. The vivid image from my dream stands in stark contrast to what I see on the news and in my community. The air is thick with tension, not unlike the scene I wrote at the beginning of my book:

"The revolution has begun!" he shouted, his voice echoing off the walls. "We will not be silenced any longer! Today, we take back our country!"

I can't help but wonder if we're heading toward a future of upheaval reminiscent of the insurrection I described. The scenes of rebellion and the cries for change echo in my thoughts. Are we destined to repeat the chaos and turmoil of the Hitler era, or can we find a way to steer toward the unity and peace of Unityville?

Hating other groups is like throwing stones into a calm pond, creating ripples that disturb the entire surface. When we let hate guide our actions, it divides us, making it harder to work together and solve problems. Hate can turn neighbors into strangers and communities into battlegrounds. It furthers misunderstanding and mistrust, which leads to conflicts and even violence. This division weakens society as a whole, preventing us from seeing the shared humanity in one another. Instead of building bridges, hate creates walls, cutting off communication and cooperation. By choosing to embrace kindness and understanding, we break down these barriers and create a world where everyone feels connected.

The contrast between my dream and the current reality is stark. But perhaps, just maybe, there's a glimmer of hope. Maybe the dream of Unityville can inspire us to strive for a better future and embrace the values of trust, community, and genuine connection that make Unityville so ideal.

As I ponder these thoughts, I feel a renewed sense of purpose. Perhaps it's up to each of us to bring a piece of Unityville into our lives and communities. To unite and create a world where unity, truth, respect, and understanding prevail.

A SHARED VISION AND COMMON PURPOSE

As you reflect on the scenes of Unityville, certain aspects may touch you deeply. Maybe it's the sense of community, the joy of creative work, the trust and mutual respect, or the commitment to lifelong learning. Whatever speaks to you, know that you have the power to bring a piece of Unityville into your own life and inspire positive change around you. And with thoughtful decision-making, you can take action that aligns with those values and leads to meaningful results.

Building Community

If the sense of community in Unityville resonates with you, start by getting to know your neighbors. Organize an outdoor movie night or a block party where everyone shares food and stories. Create a neighborhood group where people communicate and offer help to one another. The choices you make to engage with those around you can shape the supportive network you envision. For those who want to make decisions that foster deeper connections, having a framework for thoughtful decisions can guide you every step of the way.

Embracing Creativity

If you're inspired by the joy of creative work in Unityville, consider starting a community art project. It could be a mural, a garden, or even a series of workshops where people learn and create together. Making decisions on where to focus your creative energy can be easier when you have a clear sense of purpose and direction. The more aligned your choices are with your vision, the more impact you'll create in your community.

Modeling Trust and Respect

If the trust and mutual respect in Unityville stand out to you, strive to cultivate these values in your interactions. Be someone who listens deeply and seeks to understand others. When conflicts arise, approach them with an open mind and a commitment to finding common ground. By making thoughtful choices in how you handle each situation, you strengthen trust and respect within your community. Applying principles of mindful decision-making helps you stay focused on creating positive, long-lasting relationships.

Lifelong Learning

If you're moved by the commitment to lifelong learning in Unityville, take steps to further a culture of curiosity and education around you. Whether mentoring someone or creating study groups, the decisions you make to invest in education can transform lives. By being intentional about your learning journey, you inspire others to grow alongside you, making every choice a step toward shared wisdom and curiosity.

Sustainable Living

If the sustainable living practices in Unityville resonate with you, begin by making small, intentional choices in your own life. Reduce waste, recycle, and support local, sustainable products. The more mindful you are in making these decisions, the greater the positive impact you'll have on your community and the environment.

Acts of Kindness

If the spirit of kindness and support in Unityville touches you, look for ways to make kindness a daily practice. Volunteer at local shelters, food banks, or organizations that support those in need. Simple decisions—like paying for someone's coffee or offering a kind word—can create a ripple effect of positivity. These small, thoughtful choices help build the compassionate community you aspire to be part of.

Leadership with Integrity

If you're inspired by the wise and compassionate leadership in Unityville, take steps to insert these qualities into your own life. Lead by example, showing integrity in your actions and decisions. Be transparent and open and encourage others to do the same. Whether in a formal leadership role or not, your behavior will inspire others to act with honesty and compassion. Join local boards, councils, or organizations where you can influence positive change and advocate for the greater good.

As you strive to embody these values, remember the importance of seeking truth. In today's world, where information is abundant but not always accurate, it's crucial to question the source, especially when something sounds preposterous or too good (or bad) to be true. Before accepting or sharing information, take a moment to investigate its credibility. You contribute to a more informed and thoughtful community by being discerning and not spreading disinformation. The **Mindful Decisions in Motion** 5-Lesson Course offers practical guidance for those seeking to align their decisions with long-term goals, making it easier to move forward with intention and confidence.

bit.ly/mindfuldecisions

At the same time, it's important to give others a break. We're all human, and we all make mistakes. When someone falls short or spreads incorrect information, approach the situation with compassion and understanding. Forgive, offer guidance, and encourage a genuine dialogue about the truth. This not only helps correct the mistake but also fosters an environment where people feel safe to learn and grow from their errors.

Compassion and forgiveness are powerful tools in building a community that reflects Unityville's ideals. Being genuine in your interactions, admitting when you're wrong, and showing empathy toward others will encourage those around you to do the same. Remember, the goal isn't perfection but progress. Every act of kindness, every moment of understanding, and every effort to seek and speak the truth brings us closer to the connected, thriving community we all desire.

Don't just view this book as principles others should adopt and an unattainable utopia. Choose aspects of Unityville that resonate most with you and take action; you will help bring the dream of a connected and thriving community closer to reality. Each small step you take contributes to the greater good and inspires others to do the same. Together, we can create a world where the ideals of Unityville are not just a dream but a living, breathing reality.

DO SOMETHING!!

Take action and boldly express your purpose. The world needs your talents and gifts. Use them, and perhaps ... *Allied, we can find common ground for the common good.*

EMBRACING TRANSFORMATION
WITH THE NEW YOU BY DESIGN SYSTEM

As we reach the end of this journey, it's clear that spiritually centered leadership requires a deep commitment to self-awareness, vulnerability, and integrity. Each chapter has explored essential qualities that lead us toward a more compassionate and connected world. Now, it's time to take these principles and apply them to your own life, beginning with a process of personal transformation.

The **New You by Design System** is not just a tool for self-improvement—it's a roadmap for embodying the qualities we've discussed: being self-aware, mindful, compassionate, genuine, and accountable. It offers a structured way to rediscover your core values and integrate them into your daily life, helping you step fully into your authentic self and lead with purpose.

bit.ly/newyoubydesign

Throughout this book, we've talked about the importance of understanding who you are, being vulnerable in your leadership, and showing compassion to others. The New You by Design System helps you put these values into practice by guiding you through a process of re-discovery and alignment. You'll challenge limiting beliefs, uncover the values that matter most to you, and take actionable steps toward living a life that reflects those values.

This system goes beyond introspection; it's designed to help you create a new identity—one that's rooted in spiritual clarity and personal accountability. It empowers you to lead with confidence while also being compassionate and forgiving toward yourself and others. As you move forward, you'll find that these qualities naturally become part of how you lead and engage with the world.

By embracing the New You by Design System, you're choosing to live a life that validates your values and affirms the importance of human connection. Together, we can continue to create common ground for the greater good, building communities where integrity, accountability, and compassion are at the forefront of leadership.

Allied
WE CAN FIND
Common Ground
FOR THE
Common Good

BIBLIOGRAPHY

https://www.prnewswire.com/news-releases/is-the-world-becoming-more-spiritual-301458427.html

https://www.forbes.com/sites/forbescoachescouncil/2022/09/15/what-does-it-mean-to-be-a-spiritual-leader-in-the-workplace/?sh=5b41e98a538d

https://hbr.org/2018/01/self-awareness-can-help-leaders-more-than-an-mba-can

https://www.gottman.com/

https://www.ccl.org/articles/leading-effectively-articles/how-to-lead-a-collaborative-team/

https://online.hbs.edu/blog/post/how-to-lead-effectively

https://www.harvardbusiness.org/wp-content/uploads/2021/02/HBR_2020_12_compassionate-leadership-is-necessary-but-not-sufficient.pdf

https://www.imd.org/reflections/corporate-social-responsibility-csr-types-benefits-more/

https://greatergood.berkeley.edu/article/item/the_new_science_of_forgiveness

https://www.bps.org.uk/psychologist/forgiveness

https://www.hopkinsmedicine.org/health/wellness-and-prevention/forgiveness-your-health-depends-on-it

https://positivepsychology.com/psychology-of-forgiveness/

https://aguideforlife.com/recommended-resource/the-values-factor/

https://www.brookings.edu/articles/misinformation-is-eroding-the-publics-confidence-in-democracy/

https://www.cna.org/reports/2021/10/the-psychology-of-disinformation-case-studies

https://online.hbs.edu/blog/post/ethics-and-accountability-in-the-workplace

https://en.wikipedia.org/wiki/Bill_George_(businessman)

https://greatergood.berkeley.edu/article/item/compassionate_leaders_are_effective_leaders

https://en.wikipedia.org/wiki/File:Emotions.gif

ACKNOWLEDGMENTS

I have always had a great regard for history and its ability to teach us lessons about courage, leadership, and integrity. I make it a point to stay informed about current events because I care deeply about this country and the principles it was founded upon. As a proud veteran who has served in multiple ways, I love the United States, yet I've often found myself reluctant to hold up political figures as heroes. Growing up in a generation marked by scandals, it's been hard to find leaders whose actions consistently align with the values they profess.

However, the events surrounding the January 6, 2021, insurrection at the U.S. Capitol changed my perspective. Watching the country I love so dearly being attacked, not by foreign forces, but from within, was heartbreaking. It was a stark reminder of how fragile democracy can be and how essential it is to protect it. Out of the chaos, two leaders stood out to me—Adam Kinzinger and Liz Cheney—true patriots who chose their oath to the Constitution over personal or political gain.

Adam Kinzinger, a former Republican congressman and author of *Renegade: Defending Democracy and Liberty in Our Divided Country*, was one of the few in his party brave enough to call out the dangerous rhetoric and actions of President Trump and his MAGA movement. He put his political career on the line, knowing that speaking out could lead to personal attacks and professional consequences. Adam's courage in defending democracy during one of its most vulnerable moments was not just inspiring but also a call to action for me. It reminded me that in times of division, it's our duty to stand up, take action, and not remain silent.

Liz Cheney, former Congresswoman and author of *Oath and Honor*, showed similar bravery. The daughter of a former Vice President, Liz had everything to lose politically by standing up to Trump and the forces within her own party. Yet, she chose principle over politics, defending the rule of law and the integrity of our democratic process. She sacrificed her position in government to uphold her oath to the Constitution, a decision that will be remembered in history as an act of true patriotism.

This book is my response. It's a reflection on the importance of finding common ground and how to effectively stand up for what you believe in, even when it's difficult. I hope that, in its own small way, this book encourages others to have the tough conversations necessary to heal the deep divisions in our country. In a world so polarized, we need more people like Kinzinger and Cheney—people who are willing to put country over party, truth over lies, and democracy over demagoguery. They are true patriots, and I am honored to acknowledge their courage in these pages.

Contact Eric at EricMiller.us

www.ingramcontent.com/pod-product-compliance
Lightning Source LLC
Chambersburg PA
CBHW060001100426
42740CB00010B/1361